D1454286

Plato's Children

Plato's Children

The State We Are In

Anthony O'Hear

London

GIBSON SQUARE

This edition first published in the UK in 2005 by

Gibson Square
15 Gibson Square
London N1 0RD

Tel: +44 (0)20 7689 4790
Fax: +44 (0)20 7689 7395

info@gibsonsquare.com
www.gibsonsquare.com

ISBN 1 9 0 3 9 3 3 4 6 3

UK sales by Signature
20 Castlegate
York YO1 9RP

Tel 01904 633 633
Fax 01904 675 445

sales@signaturebooks.co.uk

CONTENTS

1. *The Matrix*   7
2. Shopping   19
3. Entertainment   43
4. Modern Icons   51
5. Drugs   79
6. Politics   85
7. Education   107
8. Speech Stalinism   135
9. Access   151
10. Shame   163
11. Internet   175
12. Sport   185
13. Nature   193
14. Work   205
15. Fidelity   213

Afterword   225

1

THE MATRIX

In the Hollywood blockbuster *The Matrix* we are given a story in which a man seems to be having all sorts of adventures and doing battle with all sorts of other people. In fact it turns out that all this is unreal. The hero and those he interacts with are actually all motionless in a vast laboratory. The experiences they think they are having are just images being fed into their brains by a computer, the matrix.

Perhaps not surprisingly *The Matrix* has generated a fair amount of philosophical discussion, including both a web-site and a book in which some distinguished philosophers discuss its ramifications (published by the Oxford University Press). The brains or bodies in vats, or whatever they are, who are having experiences just like us seem to pose the age-old sceptical dilemma. How do we know that we ourselves, for all the vivacity of our experiences, are not also brains in vats (or dreaming, say)? The point is that everything we do to establish the reality of our experience might just be the work of clever scientists (or of malicious demons, or part of our dream) fooling us yet again. Even the very tests we perform to show that our lives and experiences are not illusions might themselves be part of a greater illusion...

This is not a book about scepticism or indeed about philosophy. I am not going to undertake a refutation of this sort of scepticism. It would in any case be pointless, because every demonstration I produced to show that you and I were real would simply and every time be said by the sceptic to be part of the dream, itself an illusion.

But I think that another aspect of *The Matrix* plot is worth pondering. Let us suppose that things were as *The Matrix* had it, and I am and you are brains in vats, would it matter?

Would it matter from the point of view of our experiences? After all, all our experiences would ex hypothesi be the same as they are now? Would existence tied up to a matrix be worse than existence in the real world? We wouldn't know this was our situation; everything would seem the same, so would our lives and experiences be less valuable?

It is just this question which the philosopher Robert Nozick raised, also with a Matrix-like fantasy. Nozick's fantasy has the added advantage that the experiences in question would be pretty good ones, just the ones you wanted in fact. He writes:

Suppose there were an experience machine that

could give you any experience you desired. Superduper neuropsychologists could stimulate your brain so that you could think and feel you were writing a great novel, or making a friend, or reading an interesting book.[1]

Yet all the time you would really be floating in a tank, with all sorts of electrodes plugged into your brain. Let us assume that all this was a possibility. Should you plug yourself into this machine for life, programmed to have whatever experiences you wanted?

Nozick answers his own question in the negative. Most of us want to *be* something, to *do* things, to have *real* achievements to our credit, and not just to have experiences. Being tied into the experience machine we would be just an indeterminate blob, a passive recipient of experiences and also cut off from any deeper reality.

We would be in a state of perpetual illusion, as in *The Matrix*, and this in itself would be bad. In *The Matrix*, too, the audience identifies with the central character, who wants to break away from the illusion, albeit at the cost of a more difficult life. These responses suggest that deep down we do have an intuition about what is right about real life, and why illusions, even if experientially satisfying, are not ultimately satisfactory.

★★★

But the science fiction stories of Nozick and of *The Matrix* are not the first instances of the posing of the question of the relative merits of reality and illusion. Nor indeed, entwined as they are in the improbabilities of future science, are they the best or the most direct.

2,500 years ago in his dialogue *The Republic*, with his vivid image of the Cave, Plato raised just the question we are concerned with. Plato's story is a story and to that extent a fiction, but it is a story which speaks directly to the condition of each of us.

Without any mental gymnastics or discounting of technological epicycles we can easily see that the Cave might represent aspects of our own lives, here and now. And we can also see that the sort of ascent from the Cave of which Plato speaks is something which might typify our own deepest strivings, even if it is an ascent going against much of the spirit of our own times.

> Next, said I, here is a parable to illustrate the degree in which our nature may be enlightened or unenlightened.

So begins Plato's famous allegory of the Cave.[2] We are asked to imagine a group of people who are prisoners in a darkened cave. They are tied down, forced to face the back wall of the cave, and so constrained that they cannot turn their heads round to see what is behind them. What is actually behind them is a fire, and between them and the fire an elevated ramp. On this ramp there are people carrying various objects, including figures of men and animals, and moving these puppets around. All the prisoners then see are the shadows cast by the puppets on the wall in front of them. They cannot even see each other, let alone the true causes of the images on the wall. These shadows of artificial objects they take for reality.

After some long time, though, some of the prisoners are released. One of them is forced to turn round towards the fire. Initially he is hurt and dazzled by the light of the fire; he does not want to admit that what he had formerly been looking at was meaningless illusion, and tries to turn back to the wall, convinced that what was there was more real than what was really causing it. But someone drags him away forcibly, up and out of the cave, into the sunlight of the upper world.

In this state, his eyes would be even more dazzled. 'At first it would be easiest to make out shadows, and then the images of men and things reflected in water, and later on the things themselves.' And night and the moon and things of night would be easier to see than the daylight. But finally he would be able to look at the Sun and contemplate its nature, realising that it is the source of all life and activity and the cause of what he and his companions used to see.

He goes back into the Cave, into the old darkness. It takes him a while to see things in the gloom. His former colleagues scoff at him, and tell him that his sight has been ruined. If he is bold enough to try to drag him out of their unenlightened stupor, they would undoubtedly lay hands on him and kill him. (Plato's story has an obvious reference at the end to his teacher Socrates. Socrates had tried to lead the people of Athens out of their intellectual and moral confusions, but had been put to death for his pains by majority vote, which confirmed Plato in his hatred of democracy.)

In the sections of *The Republic* which follow the allegory, Plato makes various comments on it. The man who escapes from the cave will not want to go back into it. Certainly he will not want to spend all his time down there, among the unenlightened and their doings.

If he is to bring his superior wisdom down to rule the mass of people, he will have to be forced to do it. But this is just what will happen in an ideal dispensation. He will have to subordinate his own comfort and desire for the good of the rest, who will benefit from his wisdom. And we should also note that, while we do have some innate ability to get nearer the truth, the process of enlightenment is long, slow and painful.

Such is the strength of Plato's writing and the persuasiveness of his vision that most people reading the allegory will be easily convinced that there is something deeply wrong with the situation of the prisoners in the cave. And despite its implicit elitism, most readers of the story will also be convinced that they are closer to the sun than to the cave. In reading the story they have taken the first and considerable step on the road to philosophic enlightenment.

This reading strikes me as correct—in the end, and, as we shall see, with quite a bit of qualification of Plato's implicit disparagement of ordinary life.

But I also think that it is not so obviously correct that we are straightaway released from the cave simply by reflecting on the myth and finding certain tie ups with our own lives.

Indeed, I think that we can look at the situation of the prisoners in a way different from Plato's, and so that it doesn't look so bad after all.

The prisoners are, one supposes, moderately satisfied with their lot. They have what they need, a degree of entertainment and a peaceful life. Unlike the enlightened ones they do not resent being in the cave. Maybe, as the story suggests, they actually rather object if some busybody nanny (as they would no doubt see it) tries to force them to be enlightened, forces them to be free, healthy, or whatever. This, of course, would be another way of looking at the story of Socrates, looking at it from the point of view of those he annoyed and who, ultimately, condemned him to death (as much for his arrogance as for anything else, as even Plato's partisan account of the trial makes pretty clear).

And what if there is no sun, no philosophic or religious enlightenment of a Platonic sort?

In that case, aren't the prisoners actually better off than those who, painfully and unavailingly, try to drag themselves away from the admittedly base existence of the Cave? For where they are trying to go wouldn't actually exist. A non-existent sun, a philosophical will o' the wisp or a farrago of religious mumbo-jumbo, would console only by a more thoroughgoing self-deception than that undergone by the prisoners. And, if the religious teachings were those espoused by Osama bin Laden, say, this self-deception would not be one which left the rest of us unscathed or unthreatened. Cave existence, with its modicum of sense and its physical ease and security, might not in such a scenario seem so bad after all.

In contrast to the enlightened ones, in all probability the prisoners, as Plato describes them, would not develop for themselves any very systematic account of reality or their situation. In contrast to the philosophers of Plato's myth, the prisoners would not have a wholly false philosophy, conveying wholly illusory ideals, because they would not have a philosophy at all. They would simply, in a piecemeal and unsystematic way, be making the best of their situation.

If they had a philosophy at all, it would be along the lines of 'sufficient for the day is the evil thereof', combined with a desire to get as much pleasure and contentment out of each day as it comes. If there is no sun of enlightenment, could any of us do any better than that?

And maybe Plato's depiction of the Cave is unnecessarily negative. Does it have to be like a dungeon, or is he simply loading the dice to make us agree with him? Could the Cave not have some of the built-in advantages of Nozick's experience machine? Suppose what Plato calls 'the cave' were actually a bright, airy place, full of bright colours and beautiful sounds that 'give delight and hurt not'? And that, within limits, we could wander round much as we felt like. Our lives would be spent in a sort of adult nursery school, in which the worst thing that happens is that after a goodly number of trouble-free and pleasure-filled days and years, for each of us the post-lunch rest becomes a permanent state.

One could look at the history of the past few centuries, and reflect on the amazing progress we have made in all sorts of fields, from health and genetic engineering to the internet, from rapid travel everywhere to warm or air conditioned houses, from universal education to democracy and human rights, from television to cornucopias of goods in the shops.

But—and this is the question of this book—where has this inexorable drive to progress led us. In increasingly many aspects our lives resemble life in Plato's Cave. Paradoxically perhaps, our very progress drives us further into the Cave, and less inclined to make the effort to ascend from it. We cocoon ourselves in the cotton wool of fantasy, systematically turning our minds and spirits from reality. Our desires are increasingly satisfied, and, as in the experience machine, consumer choice is king.

Is this, though, what we really want? Or is the turn from reality in the end corrosive of human good?

Along with numerous many-layered evasions of reality in our lives, we still deep down (and sometimes not so deep down) show a preference for ways of being in which we come up against realities not of our choosing. Even if we were in an experientially ideal machine or Matrix state, we do not believe that this is what we should want.

Beneath the surface we do find more fulfilment in areas where our control of experience, collective or individual, is not total, and where we are happy to acknowledge powers other than our own, traditions and forms of life we did not create, and duties not cancellable at will. We do, still, within our lives, have the means to ascend from the Cave, as Plato suggests, which is another advantage of his story from our point of view over the others.

Getting out of the Matrix or the experience machine would not only be far more problematic technically, but would not depend purely on a turning of our own will and attention as Plato suggests in his parable. It is a moral turn we should be looking for, not some technological deliverance.

In a sense our situation is that described by Plato. Much of our existence is similar to that of the prisoners in the Cave; but there is a route out of it, even within our Cave, and we do have the means to struggle out of it. In the Cave, or ascending out of it; one way or the other in our journey through this life we are all Plato's children. His myth is as illuminating as any of our condition not just at 400 BC, but perhaps even more dramatically and extremely at the start of the 21st century AD.

2

SHOPPING

The Illusion of Freedom

In a famous passage the philosopher David Hume says that freedom consists in the ability to act on one's own choices, and that this freedom must be admitted to be enjoyed by everyone who is not a prisoner and in chains. Plato's prisoners are clearly unfree in Hume's sense, and we, who are not in chains, are not.

But Hume's analysis is superficial. There are other ways of being unfree than in being forced to act against one's desires. A more subtle form of unfreedom arises when one can act on one's desires, yet one remains a slave—to one's desires or to whatever wind of whim or fashion blows.

It might seem a cliché to say that the shopping mall is the cathedral of the twenty first century, but there is a point to saying it nonetheless. As the medieval cathedral was in its day, so in our day is the shopping mall the roof under which the whole community gathers. But the roof of the mall does not hang, as it were, from the heavens, raised up on the slenderest of columns, and intimating in the cavernous gloom of the single gigantic edifice a realm transcending our own. Nor do its images, constitute a Bible for the unlettered believer, referring to the mysteries of our salvation, replete with the figures of prophets, saints and the dead. Nor are its stones all hewn by hand, expressing the work and feelings of the individual craftsmen even in the imperfection of the result and in the occasional grotesquerie of the conception. Nor is its music the timeless chant of the medieval monastery or the searing, heart-rending strains of polyphonic invention.

Maybe in its apparent defiance of gravity the shopping mall reflects the cathedral of old, but there the similarity ends. For the cathedral is plainly constructed from familiar and natural materials, marble, stone, glass, wood and brick. Its defiance of gravity is the more impressive in that it is apparent that it is clearly stone which is being so raised, often on walls apparently consisting mainly of coloured glass through which shines the light of the divine spirit. By contrast the shopping mall is made of materials unknown to any but the industrial chemist, and its construction a triumph of instant technological ingenuity rather than due to the manual labour of thousands of labourers over decades, if not centuries.

Moreover, whereas in a gothic cathedral one is forever constrained by the architecture to look up, and contemplate the priceless works of God, the aim of the shopping mall is to get us to look down, at the works of man, all too easily available for a price. So while the mall may have a roof, even a transparent canopy, of which one is occasionally aware, encompassing the whole, this awareness is but a temporary respite from the main business. Once within the mall, one's eyes are continually drawn to the horizontal, by the flashing lights and competing displays of the individual stores. Once inside a store, one's senses are continually assaulted by the insistent throb and noxious wail of piped pop music, just as one's spirit is oppressed by the lowness of the roof, the harshness of the artificial light and the garish pandemonium of slogans and logos attending even the most ordinary of products.

These effects are, of course, well known to interior designers, who set things up purposely to induce in visitors to the mall a form of restlessness verging on mild panic. This makes them the less prone to tarry and contemplate, and the more prone to buy and then escape, their arms laden with purchases they do not really need and did not really want.

Consumption, self-display and choice are what shopping malls are all about, in contrast to the prayer, sacrifice and obedience of the cathedrals.

Hume spoke disparagingly of 'the monkish virtues', 'celibacy, fasting, penance, mortification, self-denial, humility, silence, solitude'. He also wrote that 'a gloomy, hare-brained enthusiast, after his death, may have a place in the calendar; but will scarcely ever be admitted, when alive, into intimacy and society, except by those who are as delirious and dismal as himself.' He doubtless has a point about a certain sort of asceticism, though whether so life-denying a spirit as he pictures could have produced so life-affirming effects as the cathedrals and seats of learning of the middle ages, or indeed the baroque of the counter-reformation, is certainly open to question.

What is equally open to question is whether the shopping mall is a life-affirming phenomenon.

This is not to say that the absence of choice and consumption, which we had in the Soviet bloc prior to the fall of the Berlin Wall, would not be petty and irksome. I well remember a visitor to this country in the late 1970s from what was then Leningrad. She could not believe that when my wife went from London to Manchester to meet her on a free day that she had not had to get official permission for the journey. She clearly suspected what would have been the case had the situations been reversed, with her going from Leningrad to Moscow to see my wife, that my wife was on some sort of semi-official mission to spy on her.

But this same visitor was also amazed to count 65 different varieties of cheese in one British shop. She wondered basically what it was for. Here one can have more sympathy with her question.

On the whole, the differences between products in the same category are small and superficial. There are a number of basic types of cheese, but hardly sixty five. The differences are even less real when we come to mass produced products like football shirts or trainers. No doubt in a sports shop there will be at least sixty five varieties of each. But the differences will be made up almost entirely by superficial factors like team colours, player's names or trade marks. The days when one might expect to be paid for enduring the vulgarity of wearing an advertising slogan are long gone. Now it is the privilege of having a trader's name emblazoned on one's breast that one pays for, and this has very little to do with the intrinsic quality of the garment. Consumer choice, vaunted as it is, reduces to the self-display of being identified with a brand name. The style one pays for is nothing more than the badge of the producer.

When Adam Smith extolled the values of the market, and of the beneficent effects of the multiple interactions between producers and consumers, this is hardly what he had in mind. He spoke of butchers putting the best meat on one's table at the lowest cost. He did not envisage generations of young and not so young people so bereft of imagination that choice reduces to paying for the name of a brand or to following the edicts of style gurus or the slogans of television advertising. He did not envisage the shopping mall replacing church or school as the heart of the community, nor the global franchise assuming in our time the authority of the classics in his. Nor, I imagine, did he envisage parents giving their young children not their time and attention, but amounts of £100 a week or more to spend on designer clothes and other accessories they do not need.

Smith did not think of the market or consumer choice or indeed consumption as ends in themselves. He saw these things as ways of enabling people to pursue other ends, which were not necessarily those we chose or, if we had chosen them, which were not justified simply because we had chosen them. Yet choice, empty choice, has become a dominant factor in the Cave, uprooting us yet more from the true realities of life. Going way beyond the operation of the shopping mall, choice has indeed become critical to the way we conceive personal relationships and even birth and death themselves. It would be only a slight exaggeration to say that in the twenty-first century birth, death and copulation are themselves seen in terms of market choice and as fit subjects for the deployment of consumer preference.

Many, if not most of our key relationships are not freely entered into. We cannot choose our parents or uncles, aunts or grandparents. As children we do not usually chose our school. Nor do we choose our place or country of birth. Even when we chose a profession or career, there is much about its structure and hierarchy and standards which are not of our making or choosing. And although there is a sense in which we may chose our children, there is a far deeper sense in which we do not chose the duties and commitments which arise from their existence once they are alive and which obtain regardless of our preferences or decisions.

Many of us try to ignore these facts or to play them

down. We think and act as if the human world is far more
plastic and malleable than in fact it is. We behave without
reverence or piety to those conditions of our world
which are not of our choosing. We tend to treat them as
if they are things which we can adopt or not, at will.
Social and physical mobility give the impression that relationships of family, birth and country are disposable, and
that loyalty is an optional virtue, the more valid for having
arisen from conscious choice. In fact, the opposite is true.
Loyalty and its benefits, like the benefits of family and
origin, arise precisely because they are there, inevitably,
unchosen, not subject to choice and hence not subject to
whim or arbitrary abrogation.

All this goes against the spirit of the age, and it goes
against the spirit into which most people enter what
they call relationships, that is what we are now known as
'partnerships' of a sexual nature. Partnerships are
obviously more than brief liaisons or affairs. They are
attempts to have the advantages of a stable marriage,
without the costs or conditions. They do not even have
to involve a man and a woman, for they can be of a
homosexual nature. Indeed part of the motivation for
talk of partnership seems to have originated with
attempts by the gay lobby, successful as they turned out,
to give homosexual relationships the same standing as
heterosexual marriage. Nor do the partnerships in this
new dispensation involve any sacred commitment or
communal sanction, a point on which many heterosex-
uals, including many feminists, would join forces with

homosexual activism. 'Partnerships' are in fact an attempt to reconfigure marriage as if it were a contract subject only to the separate and continuing consent of each of the contractors. Or to put it another way, a partnership of this sort is something which consenting adults can drop in and out of just as either party wishes, and providing that neither party feels oppressed by its continuing existence.

Thus Anthony Giddens, a sociologist and the thinker behind the 'Third Way', speaks in a book entitled *The Transformation of Intimacy*[3] of a new (New Labour) era in which sexuality becomes 'plastic'. Androgyny (or, presumably, bisexuality) is taken as evidence of the democratisation of sexual relationships. In the future a sexual relationship will be a situation in which 'a social relation is entered into for its own sake, for what can be derived by each person from a sustained association with another; and which is continued only in so far as it is thought by both (note) parties to deliver enough satisfaction for each individual to stay within it.'

There are, of course, overtones here of the famous slogan of the sexual revolution of the sixties: 'Do whatever you want, provided you do not hurt anyone else'. Only the spirit of a Giddens 'partnership' seems to be 'Do whatever you want, provided you do not hurt yourself'. *Both* parties have to consent for a relationship to continue, which seems to mean that one can unilaterally cancel it. In either case, the underlying impulse is that a life-long and open-ended commitment like marriage is inherently oppressive, inherently restrictive of freedom.

The complaint, whether feminist inspired or more general, is not without force. To bind oneself or another to a commitment 'till death us do part' does restrict freedom (and even more if the commitment is not of one's own choosing in the first place, as in arranged or forced marriage, or if it goes against one's inherent sexual orientation). People in a state of traditional marriage can certainly feel oppressed, for all sorts of reasons; and sometimes they really are oppressed, just as children can be oppressed by their parents and just as individuals can be oppressed by their neighbours and stifled by the demands of their neighbourhood.

The question, though, is whether it is right to go to the other extreme and to conceive sexual commitment on a wholly voluntary basis, without public sanction, obligation or support.

To think that it should flies in the face of some basic facts of human nature. In the first place there is what might be called the asymmetry of desire between the contracting partners, more specifically that the man and the woman might be wanting very different things from the partnership. The man might be wanting sexual favours from the woman, and, in return, the woman might be wanting children and the stability of a home and of a long-term relationship, in which to bring up the children. Both may eventually benefit from such a relationship, but in ways they cannot initially envisage, and which would be undermined were the relationship cancellable at the will of either party, regardless of the wishes of the other.

Even in the early stages, the fact of being in a commitment he cannot walk away from may give an initially rootless and potentially aggressive young man a form of stability and status which actually benefits him. But this benefit would not be available were he able—as happens now—simply and at whim to walk away from his 'partner' (and, all too often, their child or children). There is also something to be said for a man and a woman making a life together, in partnership, though not in the modern sense. In doing so and in formally joining themselves to the extended families on both sides of the partnership, they will, in their own small way and in their own lives, be replicating that sense of society itself as a partnership between the living, the dead and the yet unborn.

A partnership such as this, undertaken with irrevocable intent and publicly recognised and reinforced can also provide a unique setting of mutual consolation and support throughout life, making both parties stronger and more secure than they would be on their own. But such a thing is difficult. Where either or both parties can summarily agree to its dissolution, at will and for whatever reason, as in 'no fault divorce', the partners will have little encouragement to work through what might initially seem insuperable difficulties, but which might, were they to work them through together lead to both parties and the partnership being stronger.

No doubt initially in many a sexual relationship both

parties simply want to possess the other, in isolation from the world and in the intensity of mutual privacy, shutting out the day and all its cares. But, whether the state of loving infatuation, rightly celebrated by the poets, is a madness or not, as Plato argued that it was, it cannot last on that level. It is no basis for anything as mundane as a 'partnership' or anything as stable as marriage is intended to be.

Any partnership which is predicated on the love of a *Tristan* for an Isolde is bound to fail, as Wagner shows us with telling force and clarity, which is why in that case both parties preferred death to life. Even life together on a more worldly basis would not work, because life inevitably leads to a dilution of the sort of intense, but essentially impermanent love they were transformed by. So, a model to anyone ever subject to intense sexual infatuation (all of us, in other words, at some time or other), they preferred the madness of night and death to the daylight of life and social existence.

Wagner knew all this well enough; and having excogitated *Tristan*, *Meistersinger* was the necessary corrective, even as his own two wives both ended up sharing more of the characteristics of Wotan's Fricka in *The Ring* than of Tristan's Isolde. And in *Meistersinger* itself, is there not a hint of the calculating wife in Walther's Eva even before he wins her, as she and Hans Sachs set up Walther's victory, which in truth is more theirs than his?

If a relationship or partnership, rather than intense

sexual love, is what is wanted other factors than the pure desire of the partners must be brought into play. Choice must be constrained by commitment, and by a type of commitment which is able to persist through difficulty; through the dimming of desire, to be sure, and through temptation too, but also through such natural and inevitable facts as ageing, work, financial difficulty, strife, personal and public, sickness, tragedy, and, above all through the problems involved in the raising of children. For we should not conceive relationships without also considering the children they produce. For that reason alone, most sexual 'partnerships' must be seen as wider in scope and significance than can be contained in the desires of the partners.

At the very least, if being brought up in a stable two-parent heterosexual family by one's biological parents is what overall is best for children, then the stability of the family is not merely the private concern of two partners. That this is so has been amply demonstrated by a number of large scale studies in the USA: children who live apart from one parent are twice as likely to drop out of high school, two and a half times more likely to become single mothers and 1.4 times more likely to drop out of school and out of work, while those who live in single parent or step parent families are two or three times more likely to suffer from physical or behavioural problems than those who live with their biological parents. The stability of marriage concerns the fate of the children intimately and hence, though less intimately, the rest of the community.

But when children themselves are increasingly seen as commodities, this may be hard to appreciate.

A few years ago Mrs Diane Blood, a young widow, went to court to be allowed to become pregnant with her late husband's sperm without his explicit permission. At the time such a procedure was forbidden in Britain by the regulations then governing fertility treatment. Mrs Blood received widespread sympathy at the time. Her situation was undoubtedly tragic. She and her husband had wanted children, but had been denied the possibility by Mr Blood's untimely death. She wanted to commemorate her husband in the most enduring way possible. And she also wanted a child for herself.

One thing which the Blood case highlighted was the fact that children can now be produced outside of nature, outside of sexual intercourse. Of course, this was something we have known for two decades or more, ever since IVF treatment became possible and available. For many infertile couples, desperate for children, IVF has been a great blessing. As such it has received much favourable publicity, and its pioneers have been rewarded with honours. What, though, has not received so much attention is the fact that for every live embryo implanted by IVF five or more others are created—and then destroyed as being surplus to requirements.

Did Mrs Blood have a right to her late husband's

child? Was she right intentionally to bring a child into the world fatherless? Fatherlessness is a condition many are brought up in, and often with success, but it is usually regarded as a tragedy (like childlessness). Should one bring it about deliberately, even for the best of motives? Should that choice really be available, or is it a travesty of the human condition?

Childlessness is an affliction for many. But is it right to prevent it by means of the deliberate creation and destruction of embryos outside the womb and outside normal sexual intercourse? An interesting corollary of our tolerance of IVF treatment is that, in current discussions of embryo experimentation the point is often made that we already create and destroy embryos for the treatment of individual cases of fertility, so why should we not allow it for the promise of universal medical benefits?

Mrs Blood could not be accused of having a consumerist attitude to the child she eventually had. But this could not be said of at least some of the participants in another recent case which highlights just where we might be heading once the unnatural producing of children is both possible technically and permissible legally and morally. Where there was once a clear set of moral obligations, in which parents would not normally contemplate abandoning the children they had intentionally brought into the world, now we seem to be making up the rules as we go along and as new and hitherto unthought of situations arise.

A wealthy Italian couple, who were infertile, had

already had a child by means of surrogacy and they wanted another. The father was fair in colour and they wanted a child who would also be fair. So they found a sperm donor agency in Denmark (for a fair sperm donor) and a clinic in Athens where the implantation would be carried out. A surrogate mother was found, in whom the fertilised egg would be implanted. She was a woman from Birmingham, who had already had a number of children by different men and by different means (having already been a surrogate mother before). However, early on in the pregnancy, it was found that the surrogate mother was actually carrying twins. The commissioning parents demanded that she have an abortion, and refused to have anything more to do with the case. The surrogate mother, however, refused to have an abortion, and eventually twin girls were successfully born. She looked to have them adopted, as she could not look after them herself. Eventually she found a lesbian couple in Hollywood who wanted them, which is where they went...

This is an extreme story on all sorts of levels, and it will be said that most cases of IVF and surrogacy are not like that. Nevertheless the story does bring out in stark relief the world which looms before us once we de-couple procreation from sex. By means of easy and widespread contraception, sexual activity is already de-coupled from procreation and, as a result, has become increasingly de-mystified and purely recreational in intent, although without altogether freeing it from the passions, heartaches and jealousies it has traditionally inspired.

Recreational sex is, in fact a misnomer, or better a case of persuasive re-definition, attempting to decouple sex from any deeper feelings. One might with some justification argue that this trivialises sex, which, after all is not as a trivial matter as having a chocolate or a warm bath. If it were, people would not want it so much. But wanting the end, without the seriousness of the means, they then deprive themselves of the very thing which makes it meaningful and desirable in the first place, which at the very least involves the exploration of another person, and not just his or her body. We all know deep down that there is something wrong with Philip Larkin's adage that sex is so perfect a feeling that it is a shame to share it with another. But it is not just that masturbation is not a real substitute for sex. Sex itself is almost always more than mutual masturbation. Feelings, on one side at least, are almost always involved. Calling a relationship recreational cannot and does not eliminate the involvement of feeling and desire, and the possibility, if no more, of possessiveness, jealousy and hurt. Recreational sex is a fantasy in more ways than one.

But now it is not simply that we can have sex without babies; we can have babies without sex. And if, as seems all too likely, human cloning becomes possible we will be able to have babies without two physical parents.

This is a potentially disturbing trend, however well-meaning and closely regulated our initial forays into this region might be. For so many of our institutions and expectations regarding children are built on the natural order of procreation and childbirth. We expect children—in the main and ideally—to be born out of the love of a stable and married heterosexual couple, and to be born naturally as a result of that love. We expect them to be born to the mother who undergoes the pregnancy, of the father who lives with the mother, and in the time when both are still able to produce babies and bring them up. The upbringing of human children is a long and arduous process, best conducted by two parents in a stable relationship, and the success of many adoptions notwithstanding, by the parents who are physically responsible for the children, who are emotionally attached to them far more directly than step or adoptive parents could be and whose genes the children carry. And, as already remarked, children through their natural parents are immediately embedded in a world of extended families and generations.

In a world in which fertility by artificial means becomes a right, the natural order of procreation and birth is subverted. Natural ties are hidden and identities confused within a complex maze of sperm and egg donation and maternal surrogacy. With the freezing of eggs and sperm, we can play fast and loose with the natural order of generations. With same sex parenting, the natural balance of the family is unsettled, with all that that implies for the upbringing of children and their role models. With human cloning all these problems will be greatly exacerbated, with offspring now the subject of one person's whim and vanity, and no longer the result of the love—however imperfect—of two people who then have and assume a shared responsibility for their children.

In a way we have already travelled a long way from this ideal, now that so many teenage girls, particularly in conditions of deprivation decide to have babies on their own. Their decisions are naturally influenced by the fact that they (and the fathers) know that the state will pay for the upkeep of these babies. It is now well documented that children brought up in these circumstances are likely to do badly in all sorts of ways as they grow up, educationally and behaviourally, and also that when they grow up they are likely to repeat the same cycle as their own parents, and as their grandparents had probably done too. These cycles of deprivation surely indicate that there was something to be said for a time when teenage single parenthood was not accepted as normal.

But it is not just on British council estates that there is an issue of fatherless babies. The trend for middle class career women in their 30s to have babies without men is becoming institutionalised in America where there is an organisation known as Single Mothers by Choice, which advises single women on how to become pregnant artificially. These women have often had relationships with men, but are not prepared to have children with their partners. There are clinics ready to provide these women with sperm donations and even, we are told, a reality television show to be called 'Make Me a Mum'. A feature of these arrangements is that the 'me's' who want to become single mothers are given exhaustive profiles of the sperm donors, so that they can chose the sort of donor they want.

These profiles include not just physical details, but also the tastes and careers of the donors (e.g. not a Republican, a renovator of old homes, an MBA, a violinist, a lacrosse player). There may be some confusion here about the genetic transmissibility of acquired characteristics from parents to off-spring, but no confusion about the essentially consumerist attitude to childbirth rampant in the whole project. If Evelyn Waugh were writing today, his satire might be on the Californian way of birth, rather than on the Californian way of death, though *The Loved One* might still do as his title. But one imagines, none of this will come to be a joke for the children who are being deliberately deprived of fathers and families by what it is hard not to see as the self-centeredness, if not the selfishness, of their mothers.

These things do matter, as we see increasingly when adopted children and children produced through sperm and egg donation clamour to have the right to know who their natural parents are. Nor is surrogacy simply a matter of renting a womb, as some philosophers would have it. It involves the most intimate of relationships and feelings on all sides. It is, of course, on the basis of the natural order and the feelings attendant on that order that the upbringing of children and ultimately the stability of society is based. When having children becomes simply a matter of choice, outside the natural order, all this is threatened. It may be felt that a few individual choices of individual parents, for surrogacy, for donor insemination, will not make much difference. But once the ties are cut, the whole structure looses its stability and ineluctability.

A similar point should be made about the genetic engineering of babies. Genetic intervention to ensure that children have certain desired characteristics, or do not have certain undesired ones, elevates parental or social choice over nature in a radical way, arguably in too radical a way. For it ensures that only children meeting certain specifications are born.

In a way, we already do this (which is not, of course, a reason for doing even more of it, in a more extreme way). We routinely screen foetuses in the womb for conditions like Down's syndrome, spina bifida and Huntington's chorea. We do this, we say, so as to enable the prospective parents to choose; but the only real choice at that stage is whether to abort the foetus or not. If a woman were opposed to abortion, she would not have an amniocentesis (a procedure which itself carries a high risk of inducing a spontaneous abortion). The upshot is that large numbers of babies with the undesired conditions are aborted. Parental choice—not to take on the problems of having a handicapped child—is here elevated above the life of the child. (And, in counselling, parents in this predicament are often told that they can always have another child.) In a broad sense, this amounts to a form of eugenics, choosing only to have children of a certain type, and ensuring by one's choice that a child of a particular type is not born.

Mothers undergoing amniocentesis are not monsters, nor would be those parents who went in for the genetic modification of their children were such a thing possible and available. Parents generally want the best for their children, as do the doctors who advise and help them, and the scientists who are pioneering genetic research. So any potential parent offered the chance to have a healthy, intelligent child, as opposed to a disabled or mentally handicapped one would opt for the former. The fact that many severely handicapped people do, on their own account, live worthwhile and satisfying lives, despite their handicap, is rarely mentioned in these discussions. The stress is on the hardships and on the replaceability of this child with another. Nor is it said that many families with handicapped children develop exceptionally strong and loving bonds with them.

But suppose handicap could be removed in utero, by genetic means, rather than by abortion. The motivation to do so would be that much stronger if the desired outcome could be achieved by genetic intervention on the child who already existed rather than, as at present, by means of abortion now and another baby later.

In the individual case, the argument for parental choice of genetic manipulation of a potentially handicapped foetus, were it permitted, would be well-nigh irresistible. Given a choice, every parent would want the best for his or her child and also the best child. But before concluding that the matter is thereby settled, we need to look at the long-term consequences of allowing such choice and such manipulation as policy. And we should also reflect on why it is that disabled groups are often wholly opposed to any such thing.

Let us assume that genetic intervention allows parents, as individuals, to engineer their children in various ways. This will ensure that all kinds of diseases and handicaps are programmed out of them, even before they are born. In a society where such practices are common, handicap will not just be much rarer than it is now. It will come to be seen as something preventable, something indeed which should have been prevented had the handicapped person's parents have acted with full responsibility. Ineluctably, and without wanting it, handicap will carry far more of a stigma than it does even now. There will be talk of hard-pressed resources being spent on things which should have been prevented (that is, on people who should not have been allowed to exist).

Maybe there will also be even more talk of the quality of life of the handicapped, now by definition more rare than now. The distance between the handicapped and the fit will seem all the greater, and from the point of view of the norm, their quality of life of the handicapped so much the worse. It is not beyond the bounds of possibility that in such a society philosophers and administrators will start asking questions about whether certain types of life are worth living, and whether those living them should not be assisted, painlessly, to bring them to an end. (That this is not pure *Brave New World* fantasy is indicated that there are already quite a number of influential philosophers asking such questions and making such proposals even now regarding very severely disabled people. Plato too, following Spartan practice, wanted unfit infants destroyed, in secret; no new idea or practice this; our secret disposal involves their not being allowed to be born at all, but we might have thought we had advanced beyond the cruellest of customs of the most militaristic state of ancient Greece.)

Nor, once the genie is out of the bottle, will the definition of handicap be confined to what it is today. If and when it becomes possible to engineer genetic traits in individuals, it will no doubt be possible to ensure characteristics such as beauty and intelligence in various ways. Won't parents inevitably chose beauty and intelligence for their offspring? Nor would they be wrong to do this in the individual case. But by encouraging the operation of individual choice in this way, we will produce a society of more beautiful and intelligent people—and consequently less tolerant of the less beautiful and the unintelligent. We will move towards a more homogeneous and less tolerant society, neither of which is desirable on any level. In our individual choices for our future children, we may over-estimate the specifically human value of traits like beauty and intelligence, neither of which is particularly well correlated with either happiness or morality.

As things stand, we see people alive with all kinds of difference of health, intelligence, beauty and many other characteristics. Geneticists tell us that there are many advantages to be derived from a rich and mixed gene pool, partly because genes which may be of no use in some circumstances may turn out to be vital for survival when circumstances change. There are also great dangers in changing the genetic basis of a population, because we may not understand the long-term effects of doing so. But it is not just for reasons of biology, important as these reasons are, that exercising choice over the nature of our children is a path fraught with danger. Socially and humanly a race of genetically chosen supermen would not just be a dully uniform society, like some continuous episode of Baywatch, though it would be that; it would also be a society in which certain basic human values like sympathy and respect for the afflicted would become highly problematic. And given that, whatever form of life we live, the reality and fragility of human existence, however hedged about by genetic screening and other forms of protection, means that we will all in the end or at some time become dependent on others in all sorts of ways, mental and physical, this is a prospect which should fill us with dread. Individual choice conspiring to circumvent the realities of human existence will make that existence that much the worse for us all.

3

ENTERTAINMENT

In Plato's Cave, there is plenty of entertainment. Indeed, given that the prisoners' condition is that they do nothing but look at the shadows on their wall, it could be said that in the Cave there is nothing but entertainment. There is no reason why they should have found this an oppressive prospect, at least on the surface, providing that they like the entertainment offered. After all, our children quite willingly spend between 20 and 40 hours a week watching television, videos or the internet or playing computer games (some of these electronic hours even take place in school). Many adults approach the same levels of passive consumption of the electronic media, again quite voluntarily and without complaint.

Most of television and most of what is watched is completely mindless and deliberately so. That there have been some intelligent programmes on television is undeniable, but they were always in the minority, and never that much watched in any case. Not that could one imagine a present day Kenneth Clark (if there were one) presenting a series called 'Civilization'. The very title, let alone the tone and content would be considered far too elitist, with its Euro-centrism and implications of hierarchies of quality. The occasional televisual forays into culture these days have to be fronted by some 'personality' or eccentric in order to soften any appearance in them of judgmentalism. And instead of the words of an artist like Michelangelo simply being quoted, they are intrusively dramatised by actors after the narrator has already made the same point. This is presumably to avoid any sense of a lecture or of a 'talking head' occupying the screen. The viewing public must never be allowed to conclude that it is, in the end, they who are being judged by the great works of the past and not the other way round or that there might be something which they actually have to listen to and concentrate on.

'Never overestimate the intelligence of the public' was said to be the adage of Don Simpson, the Hollywood producer (one of the most successful ever). It is not advice that the producers on the BBC and on Britain's other main television networks need reminding of. Nor, judging by the viewing figures, do the prisoners mind.

There are academics and cultural commentators who would deny these obvious facts. There is, notoriously, a university subject called Media Studies, in which the productions of the mass media, and particularly television, are exhaustively analysed. There are academics and English teachers in schools who are prepared to defend this questionable activity not on the grounds that it offers sociological analysis (about which would not actually take a thinker like Weber or a Durkheim very long to say all that there is to say) or on the grounds that it will provide cultural criticism of the sort in which Ruskin lambasted the vulgarity of the Crystal Palace (of which there is none), but on the grounds that the material studied is intrinsically worthwhile. Television soap operas, they tell us, are just different from Jane Austen, Dickens or Shakespeare; in themselves they are no worse and they are, in addition, more relevant to pupils of today.

We are reminded here of the adage of the philosopher F.H. Bradley, to the effect that the man who thinks that 'Roses are red and violets are blue' is the equal of a Shakespeare sonnet must be either a fool or an advanced thinker. In case we are dealing here with advanced thinkers rather than fools, perhaps it should be pointed out that while Dickens can certainly be entertaining and at times verges on sentimentality, and some of his characters are definitely low, his novels as a whole are never boorish or vulgar or low. They do not track down to the lowest taste; rather, they transcend mere entertainment. They often achieve that intent and purpose which can arise only from the sustained application of a sensitivity, a morality and an intelligence beyond the norm. They teach the reader to see and appreciate things which would otherwise be invisible, and to judge their lives by stricter and more penetrating criteria than they might otherwise be inclined to apply. Rather than conforming to popular prejudice or taste, they challenge and elevate them.

They are never violent, sentimental or sensational for their own sake, unlike the characteristic productions of the mass media (including often historical reconstructions and adaptations of literary classics). Far from being ridden with cliché, they are endlessly inventive, full of ideas, of wit, of marvellous language and turns of phrase and, above all, of characters of unforgettable reality and originality. Three pages of Dickensian description (the first three pages of *Bleak House*, say) is about as far away on every level as it is possible to be from the Grand Guignol, the unremitting vulgarity and oafishness, the laziness of thought, the poverty of language and the thinness of characterisation of EastEnders, say.

It is not coincidental that EastEnders is the BBC's flagship programme, and the very one lauded by a previous Director General as being in a position to make a significant contribution to the education of the nation and the elimination of adult illiteracy. Greg Dyke said that as part of the 'learning revolution' he was initiating in the BBC, by using the characters of EastEnders and Grange Hill 'we can fire the popular imagination and bring learning to people who thought education wasn't for them'. I do not think that by this he meant that after this 'educational' process people would stop watching his programmes.

To be able to provide a full or exhaustive critique of the output of the television would be beyond normal powers of patience and endurance. Apart from anything else one would have to watch far more mind rot than one's mental powers could comfortably tolerate. I was once asked by the *Today programme* to comment on *Celebrity Big Brother*. Watching it was rather like lifting a stone while on a woodland walk and finding beneath it a hitherto unsuspected and strangely repulsive form of insect life. There seemed in it no possibility of redemption, graciousness, elegance, beauty or nobility of spirit, which were the very things which in the nineteenth century the working classes looked for so intently in their reading and in their programmes of educational self-help.

There was certainly no language beyond the most plebeian, sneering, expletive dominated, self-pitying and reductive (though, for all I know, several of the contestants were actually public school and Oxbridge educated types, anxious to reinforce their televisual credentials as persons of the people). It was the universe of the soap opera without the plot. Much the same would have to be said about the endless chat shows, in which the inarticulate parade their psychological sores and celebrities their books and films, the celebrity chef programmes, the quiz shows, nearly all of television comedy, alternative or not, and all of youth television, which between them make up a huge proportion of the most watched television. Even 'serious' discussion programmes, chaired as they might be by grandees of the media aristocracy, have to have their token 'alternative' comedian on the team, presumably to re-assure potential viewers that they are fully inclusive and non-elitist, as demanded by the Government's Agenda.

Entertainment has become a highly porous concept. The former CBS classical record catalogue, including historic performances of Beethoven's *Missa Solemnis* and Bach's *Easter Oratorio* is now put out by a division of 'Sony Music Entertainment'. The *Missa Solemnis* and the *Easter Oratorio* entertainment? *Der Rosenkavalier*, perhaps, just perhaps, but some of the most serious and deeply religious works of our civilisation, entertainment (which does not, of course, mean that they could not in a certain sense entertain)? On the same level as pop or rap? No doubt if Sony were a publisher, Pascal's *Pensées* would be 'life-style and self-help', and the mind boggles at the thought of the BBC trying to promote a programme on that book, in the unlikely event of such a thing actually being made.

Sony's misuse of the word entertainment may be a trivial point, on the face of it, but it does point to a deeper truth. The deeper truth is that we live in a society in which there has been a systematic attempt to deny any distinction between the high arts and the low. The serious broadsheet newspapers now have sections in which, in all apparent seriousness, articles about pop figures such as Halle Berry, Eminem, Oasis and the Rolling Stones are on the same level as discussions of Bach and Beethoven, Turner and Wittgenstein. One would look in vain for anything not in English, or for any discussion of Dante, say, or Virgil or Homer which assumed in the reader any familiarity with their works.

The serious question, which cannot be raised in the Cave, is whether we admit to the existence of a world of culture and learning which might elevate the mind and heighten the sensibility beyond the norm. Putting everything, high or low, good, bad or indifferent, all as entertainment, on the same level is an attempt to deny this possibility. It is a blatant example of the 'non-judgmentalism' we are supposed to cherish. This may all be re-assuring to the Cave dweller, because it tells him he need not bother to work at culture. He can let it all wash over him, and it entitles him to sneer at anything he does not understand, and might—in his ignorance—therefore regard as pretension.

He is not altogether wrong in this. There is indeed pretension and far too much chatter surrounding the arts (high and low), but someone who has been conditioned by his culture to think that that is all there is will remain, in Oakeshott's memorable phrase, 'a stranger to the human condition'. Such a person will be forever encased in the inarticulacy, in the cliché, violence and sentimentality, and above all in the insufferable smugness and parochialism of the mental world of early twenty first century 'entertainment'. For all our talk of multi-culturalism, he or she will be deaf and blind to cultural perspectives and possibilities other than our own, higher than our own and more inclusive than our own.

Our official language conspires to hide such thoughts from us.

4

MODERN ICONS

I do not remember people talking about icons when I was growing up in Chingford, any more than they talked about charisma. Of course these terms existed. They had a sense, but it was a technical, more or less theological sense. They weren't terms dropped into everyday conversations. Certainly they weren't terms one would find in the popular press, bandied around about what we now call 'cultural icons', those world famous and instantly recognisable celebrity figures endowed with some mysterious 'charisma'.

There were, of course, people we looked up to, heroes of one sort or another. Churchill and Monty, sportsmen like Don Bradman, Denis Compton and Stanley Matthews, politicians like de Gaulle perhaps and Adenauer, and for some, like our family, Pope Pius XII. But these were substantial types, often far from glamorous, at times standing for values which even then were passing, and known for their very substantial achievements. We recognised their images, but we did not recognise them for their images. There was a sense in which they were recognisable despite their images.

Like so much else, all this changed around the 1960s. Image became critical, and so did celebrity, the two phenomena becoming inextricably intertwined. You were celebrated because of your image, while your image was recognised because you were celebrated. These were big strides on our path to the emptiness of the twenty-first century. We were beginning to fashion the shadows which would be thrown on to the wall of our cave, shadows whose largely fabricated lives and personalities would come increasingly to engage our interest, and to whose state we would increasingly aspire.

In modern iconicity you become important not because of what you did or had done, but because of where and how you appeared. What you were few knew, beyond what you appeared to be and beyond what your image projected. But that did nothing to hinder your celebrity. You—or rather a very few people—became celebrated around the whole world, largely because of the image and because of the projection and instant recognisability of that image everywhere.

There had, to be sure, been figures approximating to icons of the modern sort before the 1960s. One can think of Greta Garbo and Rudolf Valentino as, as it were, proto-icons, celebrated largely for the glamour of their image, this status being attained largely through the extraordinary power of the then young mass medium of film. Modern celebrities too are largely creations of the mass media, of film certainly, but above all, of television.

They are people who, in symbiotic fashion, have exploited the media, and the opportunities offered by the media, while at the same time being exploited by the media, satisfying its insatiable appetite for celebrity and for creating new icons. And as the media have come more and more to dominate our lives, in a veritable orgy of image and sensation, so have the celebrities on whom the media feed, by whose images we are spell-bound and from which the media make their profits.

So, from the late 1950s onwards celebrities attained fame status via the media. Or rather certain individuals became celebrities oozing charisma, just because they had become icons. JFK, Marilyn Monroe, Elvis Presley, Andy Warhol. These were the new iconic elite. As time passed, there were Elizabeth Taylor, John Lennon, Princess Diana, and now we have Michael Jackson, Madonna, Sir Elton John, Naomi Campbell, Kate Moss, Tom Cruise, the Beckhams, and behing them horders of so-called A-listers, B-listers, C-listers, and for all one knows, D-listers and E-listers, many of whom feature in magazines and television programmes designed to create and promote them.

It would be wrong to say that none of these people had any real achievements to their name. But even those, such as JFK or David Beckham, who do have real achievements to their name, have a fame and an acclaim way anything beyond those achievements can justify or bear. As is now all too apparent, Kennedy would never have been a great president, while in the opinion of many who know about these things, Beckham is a very good footballer, but not one of the greatest of all time— no Pele or Best or Beckenbauer, or, to take contemporaries from other fields, not an Andrew Flintoff or a Martin Johnson either.

What does it say about the rest of us, that we rest so many of our hopes and dreams and fantasies on such fragile foundations? And that we are so easily led to take image for achievement?

We now live in a world dominated by celebrity, and not just the big iconic names already mentioned. Many at lower levels emulate the big icons. We see phenomena like *Popstars* where complete nobodies who may not even have any musical talent are projected into stardom, tracking the creation and careers of the Spice Girls. *Big Brother*, meanwhile, creates instant celebrities out of people whose only talent is that they have exposed their talentless personalities, tawdry lives and inane opinions on television. Other celebrities rise effortlessly and without trace via weather forecasting, newsreading and programmes such as *Survivor* and *Who Wants to be a Millionaire?* No doubt, if you asked ten pupils in an average school what they would most like to be, at least nine would say a celebrity.

Most of them would doubtless imagine, Cinderella like, that such a thing might actually be possible. And in one sense they would not be wrong.

You don't have to do anything to be a celebrity. You simply have to be. Or more precisely you simply have to have a projectible image. Prince Charming will even do that for you, if only if only you meet him or her in the form of a media Svengali. But there, of course, is the rub.

The democracy of celebrity in a paradoxical way emphasises its exclusivity. Few actually get to see, or more importantly to be seen, by the all powerful pop or TV producer. It is like winning the lottery. Anyone can win it, and anyone can see that anyone can win it. But only a miniscule minority actually do. Even as our icon-dominated, celebrity-infested world creates hope in millions of youthful breasts, it breeds a tremendous cynicism and resentment in the vast majority who see that world inevitably receding far from their reach.

The celebrities have done it and they are no better or different from the rest of us. They are no different from the rest of us, except in the one crucial respect. They have made it to the promised land. And in that we are a million miles from them, as they bask in their fantasy land which the rest of us have no realistic hope of ever entering.

★ ★ ★

As with the saints of old there is a grace to be won just by coming into contact with a modern icon. This was seen in its purest form in the case of Diana. Those who met her and basked in her smile felt transformed and even at times overwhelmed almost physically. But it is true of the others too. Think of the faces in the crowds surrounding Kennedy (and even Clinton, his would-be reincarnation). Think of the mania surrounding John Lennon, like nothing so much as religious hysteria. Think of the quasi-religious reverence which attaches to Elizabeth Taylor when she enters a room.

Unlike the saints of old, who were depicted in real icons, our modern icons are not infused with holiness. But like the saints of old they are unreal human beings. In their images they are as they or their publicists would have the rest of us see them. Their aura is not that of holiness and their world is not supernatural, but they are not of the everyday world.

Their world is celebrity land, a strange half-existence as far removed from the real world as that of heaven itself. The papers sometimes delight in showing us pictures of celebrities doing ordinary things the rest of us do, Madonna shopping, say, or Tom Cruise getting out of a car. And, of course, you still have to struggle out of a car, even if it is a Porsche, and a carrier bag from Fortnum and Mason is still a carrier bag.

Actually Madonna may even go to the supermarket. She falls off a horse. These are ordinary people after all, creatures of the everyday, like the rest of us. But there is something not quite right about this. The double take makes everyone uncomfortable and we quietly forget that we ever saw the star without her make up, in ordinary lighting and a baggy sweatshirt and jeans.

At the same time, although they are not of the everyday world, they do emanate from the everyday world. They are the fantasies of the everyday. They are what the broad mass of mankind would be and would have, were their fantasies realisable.

What, after all, was Marilyn Monroe but the deification of the common place Norma Jean, the small time model launched through liberal applications of peroxide and judicious change of name and identity into Hollywood and upwards into the President's bed? Whatever talent she had as an actress, it seemed to have little to do with learning or with plainer routes to success, such as hard work and dedication to a craft.

And the President himself, remembered and known now not for his political adventures, the Cuban fiasco and the failed civil rights legislation, to say nothing of Mayor Daley's fixing of his election (in a tough, cut-throat world, a real political achievement that), but for other things altogether: his film star persona and his model star family, small town America writ glamorous—and later by the truth which was hidden behind that image.

Strangely enough, although the reality undermined the originally carefully crafted family image, if anything

JFK's iconic status has been enhanced after his death by the revelations of his sexual voracity and success. Camelot was not so much Arthur and Guinevere and the Knights of the Round Table, as Playboy Towers, the fantasy of everyman; and if not quite for everywoman, at least some could take heart and inspiration from the upward mobility of Marilyn and the rest.

It is hard, though, to live up to the fairy tale. The life of a modern icon is not as glamorous as it is made to seem. Some, indeed, have been profoundly unhappy, even committing suicide, as in the case of Marilyn Monroe, or eating themselves to death, as in the case of Elvis Presley. Most, one imagines, have periods of considerable boredom and worse.

Being an icon may indeed be tiresome at times, to say the least. If you are celebrated mainly for your image and you are at all reflective, you will come to feel inadequate to the extent that your fame outstrips your actual merits or abilities. Particularly when social excitements and adulation do not staunch them, the icon will feel periods of profound doubt and disillusionment, and may well resort to drink or drugs or ever more frenetic rounds of partying, shopping and relationships. So, inevitably, hangovers, frustrations and depressions become part of the iconic way of life.

To keep the icon from too much human reality, it obviously helps all round if he or she is dead. It is easier for him or her not to have to bear the burden of iconicity when the image fades. And it is easier for the rest of us to have the perfect image frozen in a youth never inconvenienced by age.

Removed from reality into celebrity land, modern icons are nothing if not inclusive. They must never be 'judgemental' or elitist. Because only by appearing no different from the rest of us can they be icons for everyone.

High born or aristocratic celebrities emphasise a sort of ordinariness and especially how they reach out to everyone, particularly the 'disadvantaged'. This was true enough of Kennedy, with his advocacy of civil rights and garnering of the black and working class vote. But Kennedy was a mere amateur in comparison to Lady Diana Spencer, Diana the Princess of Wales; the daughter of a family with centuries of nobility behind it, who married the heir to the throne (and, who when she needed it, never let anyone forget it).

Cynically it could be said that it was precisely Diana's birth and position which allowed her the luxury of her virtuoso-like feats of inclusiveness and non-judgementalism. But for most of the population Diana's triumph was precisely that she was all things to all persons, and never more all things to all persons than when the persons concerned might be seen as disadvantaged or marginalized.

In icon land we are not supposed to be divided. It is a

world of wish-fulfilment, in which the lion lies down with the lamb, in which all can have peace and prosperity, in which all can be equal, just by wishing it. Not for nothing is Lennon's saccharine 'Imagine' its anthem, and his infantile 'Give Peace a Chance' its battle hymn, its maudlin melody sung by a million supporters of the vicious Viet Cong. Live8 is only the latest manifestation of the magical superstition that attending a pop concert can somehow change the world (reduced in this case to complete vacuity in that the worshippers were told that all they needed to do was to be there).

In this atmosphere those who do divide us are not welcome, however much they actually achieve. They are the evil ones who remind us of things we would rather forget, like original sin, the ineradicability of inequality and the tiresome fact that the goods of the earth do not descend on us like manna from heaven.

Never was the essence of the modern icon more revealed than in the case of Andy Warhol. Warhol was himself an icon, but he was also a creator of modern iconography. In his life and work Warhol symbolised and encapsulated the essence of the modern icon. He was his striking appearance, with nothing behind the exotic surface; and he created other icons by projecting their image globally: Marilyn, Elvis, Elizabeth Taylor, Jackie O, Chairman Mao and, of course, himself.

From the artistic perspective, Warhol actually did little, as we will see, but he did show that in the celebrity-land of the Cave that anyone could be an artist. Even more he showed that art was about creating and being a celebrity. And his greatest artistic creation was himself: the artist as celebrity, the Andy Warhol everyone recognises.

Warhol was originally a moderately successful commercial artist, who then transformed himself into becoming, after Picasso, the greatest art phenomenon of the twentieth century. But Warhol was very different from Picasso. Picasso was the last of the heroic painters, in a tradition which would include Michelangelo, Leonardo, Rembrandt, Monet, Cézanne, men whose lives were consumed by their art and whose art involved new ways of seeing forged from their own perpetual struggle with their materials. One can criticise much of what Picasso did as an artist and as a man. But what one cannot criticise him for is for not being a supremely gifted and hard working transformer of materials. Whatever else he was, first and foremost he was an artist in the traditional sense. Through his continual transformation by his own hand of initially unformed materials, he communicated his imaginative visions to the rest of us, changing forever the way we see the world.

In this traditional sense Warhol was not an artist. Once he stopped his commercial work, there are few traces of the artist's hand. His most famous works are prints of (other people's) photographs produced by what are technically referred to as 'variations of photo-mechanical silk-screen processes', and mimetic representations and replicas of common-place, mass produced objects like soup cans and Brillo pad boxes. If by 'artist' we mean someone who by his own hand imaginatively transforms materials like paint and marble, in the works for which he is most celebrated, Warhol was hardly an artist at all, let alone an artistic genius. Indeed Warhol's defenders, like the philosopher Arthur Danto, take it to be part of Warhol's genius that he 'violated every condition necessary to something being an artwork, but in so doing he disclosed the essence of art.'[4]

But, if not as an artist in the traditional manner, Warhol was a genius in another sense. He incarnated perfectly in his work and in himself the modern cult of celebrity. He did this both in his representations of others (Marilyn Monroe, Chairman Mao, Jackie O and the rest) and in his creation of himself as pure celebrity. Warhol was celebrity for its own sake, celebrity in the purest sense, uncluttered by the trouble of effort or achievement in any other direction than that of celebrity itself.

According to Danto, Warhol was 'the nearest to a philosophical genius' that twentieth century art produced. This is not because of the epigrams assembled in the 1975 work entitled *From A to B and Back Again: the Philosophy of Andy Warhol* (sample: 'Diet pills make you want to dust and flush things down the john.'). It is rather because in showing that anything, just anything, could be art, Warhol disclosed the essence of art. According to Danto, Warhol brought artistic practice to a level of self-consciousness never before attained, and in doing so actually brought about the end of art. Anything could now be an artwork. No observable properties need now distinguish reality from art at all. The narrative of art history from Giotto, say, to Picasso and the abstract expressionists has now come to an end, and with it the elitism and sense of awe surrounding that narrative. As Danto puts it, 'the art gallery has been transformed from a temple of beauty to a cultural fair.'[5]

One's first reaction to all this is that it is pretentious rubbish, and to quote back at Danto one of Warhol's own disclaimers. (For example, 'I don't think that many people are going to believe in my philosophy, because the other ones are better.') But actually Danto is on to something deep, not about art exactly, but about the spirit of our age. In one of his essays on Warhol, Danto quotes Edmund White:

Andy took every conceivable definition of the word art and challenged it. Art reveals the trace of the artist's hand: Andy resorted to silk-screening. A work of art is a unique object: Andy came up with multiples. A painter paints: Andy made movies. Art is divorced from the commercial and the utilitarian: Andy specialized in Campbell's Soup Cans and Dollar Bills. Painting can be defined in contrast to photography: Andy recycles snapshots. A work of art is what an artist signs, proof of his creative choice, his intentions: for a small fee Andy signed any object whatever.

It is not, of course, true that Warhol has brought about the end of art, even in the traditional sense. Taking only the visual arts, plenty of people still paint and draw and sculpt, even if their efforts are routinely dismissed by the Warhol-invoking, celebrity-obsessed cultural elite of our age, and even if their efforts are slender in comparison to those of earlier ages. But with his relentless invocation of the images of the commercial world and of pop, Warhol has certainly done a lot to erode the distinction between a high art of serious ambition and a popular art, essentially trivial and ephemeral. This was indeed part of his agenda.

As this ambition is one essentially suited to a democratic time of populist celebrity together with low ambition and low achievement—to our time, in fact— Warhol has indeed succeeded. See, for example, the way in our broadsheet newspapers, pop music and film actresses are accorded the same respectful attention as, say, an exhibition of the paintings of Titian or a cycle of Beethoven symphonies (which will itself very likely be sold on the basis of the image of a media friendly conductor).

See, too, the recent outpourings of John Carey, Oxford Professor of English Literature and, nowadays, ubiquitous highbrow critic.[6] According to Carey art is simply 'anything that anyone has ever considered to be a work of art, though it may be a work of art only for that one person'. Art is no good, and does no good, except in so far as someone—anyone—likes it, or thinks of it as art. There is no distinction between high art and low art. There are no judgements about art or discriminations of quality which are not purely subjective.

Less stylish than Warhol, what we have here is the Warhol agenda in threadbare academic hand-me—downs. Carey appears untroubled by the consequence of his position, that if there are no genuine judgements of quality in art, then the whole phenomenon of art, including his own field of literary criticism, is reduced to the exercise of power relations. The artists who counts, like the celebrities which count, are those who have most power over the media and the critical elite, and who are most powerfully promoted by the most powerful promoters and publicists. Artists indeed are celebrities and, if we follow the example of Warhol, as perhaps we should, we might say that celebrities are artists. Celebrity is all.

As an empirical fact, this may be true of Warhol himself and of the art world post-Warhol. Nonentities, pumped up by impenetrable pseudo-academic drivel and demonstrating over and over again that indeed anything can now be an artwork, become, for a time, the darlings of the promoters and critics.

But, even if it is too obvious for Carey to see, it is a position which is, in the long term, absurd, as can easily be seen if one were to compare the output of Beethoven, say, with his not unworthy contemporary Hummel,

Titian with a salon painter like Bouguereau or today's Jack Vettriano, Michelangelo's sculpture with the installations of Emin and Hirst, Eliot's Four Quartets with the verse of Patience Strong and Pam Ayres, or Proust with Harold Robbins and Paulo Coehlo. If we follow F.H. Bradley's adage, Carey must be either a fool or an advanced thinker. Carey is not at all a fool, but he happily engages in the sort of advanced thinking which so flies in the face of all actual thought, analysis and experience that it gets thinking a bad name.

Actually Carey is not a pure advanced thinker. In his own book he shows that he is not, at least in his actual critical practice when he gets down to the detailed examination of works of art and literature. He is also right in thinking that there is no necessary connection between artistic appreciation or creation and goodness of behaviour. We should, therefore, resist any conflating of the two, or any attempt to reduce the aesthetic to the moral, overlaps between the two notwithstanding. There are different values in human experience, distinct from each other (which is not to say that there is not something peculiarly grotesque and self-contradictory about the camp commandant's attention to Beethoven).

But, on the other hand, Carey also points out the way in which appreciation of literature and music can be life affirming for people starved of these things, and also that literature 'enlarges your mind, and it gives you thoughts, words and rhythms that will last you for life'.

Given his extensive examination of the words and

rhythms of Shakespeare and other canonical writers and his often amusing descriptions of contemporary conceptual art, it is hard to believe that Carey thinks deep down that any art or any writing is equally good at enlarging the mind. At any rate mind enlargement might well be a starting point for comparative criticism of art and literature which goes beyond the narrow relativism of Carey's professed position on art. Like all relativisms, whether in morality, knowledge or art, Carey's relativism founders quickly on the rock of actual experience and actual judgement.

In a sense, though, as Carey intimates, Warhol has indeed brought about the end of art. One can now be an artist—a famous artist, the most famous artist of the second half of the twentieth century indeed, by exhibiting no traditional artistic skill, by imaginatively transforming no materials, by actually doing absolutely nothing, beyond—and this is crucial—being famous for being an artist, by being *the* art celebrity.

We should also consider Warhol's own relationship to celebrity in his work. Danto remarks that 'Warhol invented a form of portraiture that henceforward specified the way stars would appear. Everyone he portrayed became instantly glamorous by being transformed into the unmistakeable Warholesque image: Liza Minelli, Barbra Streisand, Albert Einstein, Mick Jagger.' But, and this is the point, the Warhol image factory could and did treat complete nonentities the same way: 'just as the Coke drunk by Liz Taylor is no better than the one drunk by the bum on the corner, so Chairman Mao is no more a star than Bianca Jagger, and the black and Latino transvestites of the print series "Ladies and Gentlemen" are no less—or more glamorous than Truman Capote or Lana Turner... This is how one looks in one's own fifteen minutes of world fame.'

This is the point. Warhol has triumphantly demonstrated that the artist is no longer a person of talent and skill, but that anyone can be an artist and that art is now wholly democratic. Warhol's art demonstrates that celebrity can attend just anyone whose fifteen minutes happen to coincide with the ever revolving doors of the media factory, Andy's or some other's. In an age of instant and democratic celebrity, anything is possible... Reality has nothing to do with it. Iconicity is all, with Warhol a pivotal figure as both iconic image and icon maker.

Except, of course, that everyone cannot be a celebrity, or, *Big Brother* notwithstanding, not everyone can have their fifteen minutes of world fame. They need to be, like Andy himself, a celebrity or at least a celebrity in the making. They need either to have Andy's celebrity-making talent themselves or behind them someone doing it for them.

Andy's greatest creation was his own image, the icon, behind whom there was nothing, above all there was no thought. Warhol endlessly said that he had nothing of interest to say, and people did not believe him. But they should have believed him, because what he showed was that it was possible to be just an icon; the less behind you, the more perfect your iconicity, because there is nothing to disturb the perfection of the image and nothing to divide the adoring crowds.

People sometimes complain that their fame notwithstanding, today's celebrities do not have anything interesting to say, that they can be somewhat monosyllabic, that they are not always the most scintillating conversationalists. But all this is to miss the point. Can anybody remember anything Diana said, or Marilyn Monroe or Elvis? Icons are not what they are because of the profundity of their intellect or the speed of their wit, for if they were, identification with them and their fame would be impossible for the vast majority of us. What is important is what they appear to be.

An exception here might be thought to be John Lennon. Lennon made political pronouncements and wrote poetry of a sort. But reading the stuff now, in both cases, it is quite clear that no one would have taken any of it seriously had it not been produced by someone who was not already of iconic standing (more popular than Jesus, he told us). Not to put too fine a point on it, taking the politics and poetry of Lennon seriously manifests a degree of condescension of the sort evoked by Dr Johnson in his notorious remark about a woman preaching (like a dog standing on its hind legs, the wonder is not that it is done well but rather that it is done at all). But, as befitting his iconicity, what Lennon had to say expressed the fantasies of his age, glossing over the uncomfortable realities which divide us, as did Diana in her time.

69

★ ★ ★

We live in a world dominated above all by celebrity and by image. The mass media have participated in this process to such an extent their own output is largely dominated by celebrities and the cult of celebrity. As a result our lives are dominated by figures whose reality is inseparable from their image, and whose connection with any reality beyond their image is increasingly tenuous.

Why else indeed do we spend so much time looking at the images of distinctly unfamous and untalented singers and actors? What makes us think that creatures in programmes like *Big Brother* and *Survivor* are real—when the situation is utterly contrived, and the 'reality' is that constructed by the television producers precisely to elicit tremors of sensation and prurience? There is, of course, an element of narcissism about the sort of celebrity celebrated in the modern world. In looking at these icons, we feel that we might be looking at people we might know or even at ourselves, had our phone call been the one to get through to the programme organisers.

And we also look at the world we and our media have created. It is one in which there are infinite rewards for image without substance; and this itself is a potent cocktail, creating hopeless dreams in vast numbers of ordinary people, who see themselves as essentially the same as the icons, and, when those dreams prove obstinately unrealisable, endless frustration and irritating discontent. Better perhaps a world of more solid ambition and more solid achievement. But until that occurs a few insubstantial icons will continue to project themselves on to the wall of our cave, while the prisoners, their peers in their millions will continue to gaze and dream.

And on no one do they continue to gaze and dream, and envy, more than Victoria Beckham, the quintessence of modern celebrity. In considering Victoria we will come to understand better both the nature of modern celebrity and the mechanics of its production.

In focusing on Victoria Beckham in this way, I do not mean to imply that she is exceptional in the world of celebrity or that she is in any sense malicious or unpleasant. What I want to concentrate on is the bare fact of her celebrity, which is not by any means due to her marriage, being already well-established by that time. It is precisely in her celebrity, and in what underpins it, that she is so symptomatic of life in the Cave.

Among her other achievements, Victoria has produced a best-selling autobiography, *Learning to Fly* (2002), from which many of the observations I am about to make derive. The book is extremely long and, it has to be said, for anyone not interested in the minutiae of the Spice Girls and of 'life with David', also extremely boring. But, perhaps by default and while not giving away any classified information, so to speak, it is also extremely revealing—and not just in its triumphant demonstration that there is nothing remotely posh about the eponymous Posh.

Quite early on in her book Victoria explains her approach to theatrical auditions. She was not, she says, the best singer, having been on the dancing course at Laine Theatre Arts, her theatre school. But she could always belt something out, and draw attention away from her vocals by 'doing all the moves'. In any case, 'I didn't want to showcase my voice, I wanted to showcase my personality'. Further, 'being in a pop group is not about having the best voice, it's about image and personality'.

There Victoria is speaking for all those millions of young girls who want, above all else and lacking all else, to be simply celebrities. That, as the Spice Girls were to tell us, is what they really want, really really want, and so they queue in their thousands to audition for shows such as *Popstars* and *Big Brother*. And Victoria stands for them all, and speaks for them all.

As she tells us herself, like so many of her peers, when young she was afflicted with spots and with weight. She was far from being a star at Laine Theatre Arts. Nor was she particularly popular with fellow students.

She does, of course, get her revenge and exults in it, in the authentic tones of the modern celebrity, of the *Big Brother* public confessional. Having just got a record in the top ten for the first time, our soon to be celebrated heroine reflects. She could, she says, 'just hear all those arseholes at my school, the girls who found it hard to keep their legs together, who called me names' saying that they were friends of hers, and the boys 'who called me frigid' saying they had slept with her. She adds 'Warning: if you ever hear anybody saying they were friends of mine at school then you will know that these people are lying. I'd always said I'd show them and I had.

For, despite the lack of faith shown in her by the school and her contemporaries, 'I am the most successful person who has ever come out of Laine's. It doesn't matter what you look like, it's all about hard work, determination and self-belief.' But self-belief in what, about what? In, it seems, that most elusive of qualities, personality.

We are told that at the original audition for the Spice Girls, better singers than the ultimate five were turned down 'because you need more than good voices. The Spice Girls are not only successful because of our vocals, but because of our personalities.' And even now, even when the Spice Girls are no more and Victoria is half of the ultimate celebrity partnership she does not want fame alone: 'Being famous for tottering around in high-heels and wearing designer clothes is not enough. I don't want to be famous for being famous. I want to be famous for what I do best. Performing.'

But—and this is the key to the ultimate bathos of modern celebrity—talk of performing by itself tells us nothing. There was a time and there is a type of performance in which the performer precisely loses his or her personality in the service of some work greater, less transient and more objective than his or her personality.

The performer is at the service of his or her art, and in this interchange of art and performer, both may be ennobled. But in the case of a pure performer, like Victoria, art is, as we have seen, at the service of the performer, a vehicle for the show-casing of the performer's personality. In this transaction, neither is ennobled. The art is quickly forgotten and the personality, thrown back entirely on its own slender resources, is revealed, or more likely veiled, in the cliché of soap opera or celebrity interview.

To make the point a little more specific, one could not imagine Janet Baker saying that she had succeeded because of her personality, or speaking of being famous for performing alone, or even making any remark about her 'vocals'. Dame Janet would tell you that she had succeeded, to the extent that she had, because she had suppressed her personality in the service of Mozart, of Handel, of Gluck, of Schubert, of Schumann, of Wolf—of artists in whose service one learns the insignificance of one's own unformed personality, and in whose service one also learns what, with culture and selflessness, one can become.

The point is that personality is a little thing and an uncertain thing. At no time is this more true than in adolescence, when one has glimmerings that one has a personality, but before one has been fired or tested in some way, or measured against something which is truly great. The difficulty is that at adolescence one's feelings are as strong as ever they have been or will be. They are not commensurate with any achievement or potential one might have, but, despite or because of all this, one has an overwhelming urge to express one's personality and to perform—anything, anywhere, just to be recognised. In this sense the modern cult of personality is part of our worship of adolescence.

Latching on to this, the Spice Girls or their creators did indeed, as Victoria says, conquer the world, and they did so by projecting the adolescent personality. Just as Warhol showed that anyone could be an artist, so Victoria and her colleagues seem to show is that any adolescent girl (or boy) has the potential to become an instant celebrity, apparently by doing nothing other than being what they are. (Apparently, because the reality is that a huge media effort lay behind the success, just as in the case of Warhol, and no doubt too, as in the case of Victoria, a lot of work and determination.)

Girl power was not just, in the circumstances, an inspired slogan. It is also the notion which is captured in the Spice Girls' first and most famous hit, 'Wannabe'. What 'Wannabe' says and what the girls projected was the message that if you wanted something hard enough, if, in the immortal phrase you really really wanted it, then (mysteriously) you could actually get it. On the face of it, the 'it' is 'to be my lover', but there is more than a hint that behind and beyond that 'it' is some more generalised fame or celebrity. After all, 'wannabes' are, like the Spice Girls themselves, those wanting fame, but who have yet to achieve it.

On the face of the song, the means you have to adopt if you are to be my lover is that the 'wannabe' lover has to take the girls and their friends on their own terms. Girl friendship, girl power, is more important than boy-girl love. But, from the point of view of the girls themselves, those at once accepting and refusing the lover, the means to what they want is that exemplified by the Spice Girls themselves in their performances: a flaunting of a frenetic, but trivialised sexuality, combined with a high degree of cheek (in other words, what so many 14 and 15 year old girls today take for granted as the means to get what they want).

This is the flaunting of an adolescent sexuality. It is girl power, not woman power. It is micro-dresses, bare midriffs, and in your face thrusting and gyrating, rather than veils, seduction and mystery. The Spice Girls were and continue to be imitated by countless thousands of girls even in primary school, girls who may just be becoming aware of their bodies and of the potential power of their bodies, but who have little experience of life or of love or of the complications which come in real relationships. What is at issue is a highly reductive and mechanised view of sexuality and of human life more generally, as mechanised as the music and the movement the Spice Girls used to convey the message.

The Spice Girls performances were not just mechanistic. They also contributed significantly to a culture—reflected also in teen and celebrity magazines—which can hardly be regarded as healthy. It is an atmosphere in which it is assumed that everyone, including young girls, are mainly obsessed with sex and sexuality. Up and down the country, girls as young as nine or ten, are encouraged to flaunt a side of themselves of which they may hardly be aware. Through this flaunting—performance and self-presentation—they think that they can become celebrities. You can get what you want through sex, but without any of the messiness or meaning or mystery of sex. It is hard not to see this as decadent. One has to wonder about the consistency and indeed the morality of a society terrified of paedophilia on the one hand, but encouraging its young girls to ape the Spice Girls and similar celebrities on the other.

Victoria's dream, like that of so many young people who want to be taken seriously—as performers—is that they will no longer be 'mocked for being spotty, or thick, or a rich kid who wasn't like the rest of them', or, as now, being disparaged for being famous for merely being famous. I doubt very much that Victoria Beckham is thick, but she and her career stand as a potent symbol to so many, thick and unthick unlike, that all is possible if only one can perform, can showcase one's personality, but without any reference to what it is that you might be performing. This is the ultimate wannabe's dream, the quintessence of celebrity for its own sake, and in Victoria's case both the dream and the essence have been realised.

But there is no reason to suppose that either dream or essence are ultimately more satisfying than ordinary life. They may indeed be considerably less satisfying, in that celebrities are very much creatures of the media. They have to conform to the image constructed of and for them. On stage or not, they are always performing, acting out roles which may not be them. This cognitive distance may well be psychologically troubling, leading all too often in the case of the celebrities themselves to drink, drugs and depression.

This is not the case with the Beckhams. But, as we see in the case of Victoria herself and in the endless media intrusions into her marriage, those whom the media have blown up, the media takes delight in blowing down. Even as a modern morality tale we can hardly be proud of being consumers of gossip and tittle-tattle which ruins people's lives—even if they are celebrities. To this extent one must have sympathy with the Beckhams and with all the other celebrities whom the media turn on; but in saying this, we also have to remember who the consumers of the gossip and tittle tattle are. The cult of celebrity is harmful not only to the celebrities themselves. It taints us all.

5

DRUGS

There are few more poignant images in modern life than the one we contemplate in the tabloids almost weekly: a celebrity, fed up no doubt with the emptiness and fabrication inherent in celebrity existence and having taken to drink or drugs, making his or her way to Priory Lane, Roehampton. For that is the location of a famous clinic for drug addicts and abusers, much patronised by the rich and famous. Not is there anything remotely edifying in the way Kate Moss has been pursued and pilloried for allegedly using cocaine, not just because no one seems to doubt that such practices are rife within the worlds of modelling and celebrity, but even more because of the obvious moralistic gloating which accompanied the 'allegations'.

No doubt there is an element of Schadenfreude in seeing images of riches and beauty to rags and the devastation of addiction, or in seeing a career broken because of some public revelation of drug taking. Not is there anything new in any of this: look at Hogarth's

Rake's Progress from the eighteenth century and at similar age-old morality tales. But delight in the fall of another is not only petty in itself; it is shallow as a response to what we are witnessing. It does not get to the bottom of what is wrong with drugs, nor does it explain why drugs are so potent in our time, as both lure and symptom.

We know that drugs wreck lives, and that drug addiction is terrible. Drugs are not, of course, confined to the glittering world of celebrity. Along with binge drinking they are a curse which afflicts every stratum of society, a tempting evasion of reality for whatever reason, personal or communal. Drugs and drink and their abuse have been features of most societies at most times. Our case may be different, though, both because of the extent of the abuse of drink and drunks, and in our reluctance to attach any stigma to it.

We also know that every time a new drug becomes fashionable we are assured that it is harmless. For decades this has been claimed of cannabis. In the 1960s there were articles in periodicals of informed liberal opinion telling us that cocaine was safe and clean. There are even those who would defend the credentials of heroin, provided it is clean in itself and taken in suitably controlled circumstances.

As a matter of empirical fact, all these claims have proved to be baseless. Even the apparently mild and peace-inducing cannabis weed turns out to rot the brain if taken over long periods, though whether it follows from this that it (or other drugs) should be legally prohibited is another matter.

But let us assume, for the sake of argument, that a so-called recreational drug were developed, which produces a great sense of euphoria and that it really does have no unpleasant or unhealthy side effects. Let us suppose that taking it induces all kinds of pleasant feelings, sensations and images, exciting, sensuous or languorous, as one wishes, so that people become accustomed to spending large parts of their leisure time under its influence, and do so regularly. One could imagine such a cocktail being part of the amenities of the cave, were those controlling the prisoners benevolently inclined. It was just such a role that Aldous Huxley envisaged for the drug Soma in *Brave New World*.

So, from a rational point of view, what is wrong with Soma, assuming it has no addictive or otherwise deleterious side-effects? What Soma is supposed to do is to give the subject release from all the cares of life (of which in *Brave New World* there are few enough anyway), and to enter 'the warm, richly-coloured, the infinitely friendly world of Soma holiday'. Soma is, in fact, aimed at producing that state to which mystics aspire, a state of mind completely attuned to the present; though the brave new world expression of timeless bliss lacks a little of the resonance of Julian of Norwich, say: 'Was and will make me ill, I take a gramme and only am.'

Part of what is wrong with Soma is what Huxley himself says in *Brave New World*, at least. Far from opening the doors of perception of those who take them, drugs actually raise 'a quite impenetrable wall between the actual universe and their minds'. That indeed is their point, and it also explains why in the novel the rebellious hero Bernard actually wants to be subjected to some great trial and affliction in order to be thrown, Soma-less, on his own inner resources, and also to experience the world directly in all its harshness, beauty and mysteriousness.

It is because we put so little emphasis on inner resources that drugs seem so attractive, particularly to that form of celebrity which celebrates nothing but itself and which regales itself simply in being celebrated. But there is a deeper difficulty with seeking any substantial satisfaction through drugs. It is that it mis-construes the nature of true satisfaction.

For happiness is not a sort of feeling or sensation, or even a sustained mood of euphoria. So it is not the sort of thing which can be produced or induced by drugs. Happiness is a by-product of living well or of contem-plating something beautiful or meaningful with full alertness. It is the result of having done something well or of having achieved something worthwhile.

As with empty celebrity, aiming to achieve happiness by means of drugs is an ultimately unavailing attempt to get a form of consolation without having the basis which makes the consolation what it really is. It is as if someone were to celebrate a success without having succeeded in the thing being celebrated. It deprives the euphoria aimed at of substance and meaning. Any sense of euphoria gained through drugs will be empty and short-lived, and because unsubstantial, of entirely transitory worth.

Drugs can create the illusion that real satisfaction can be had in isolation from what one is or does, and in isolation from reality. This leads to a harmful dissociation of one's source of satisfaction from the rest of one's life. In some cases, as Huxley suggests, this can have a political dimension, with Platonic implications. The prisoners in the cave are being supplied with drugs to reconcile them to their lot. But in the end it won't work. An existence whose satisfactions are drugs based is destined for the Priory or worse.

Drugs give the user the impression that the world is at his feet; in that very moment he is enslaved more completely than he is able to imagine. The ultimate lightness of the being he feels he is, is actually tethered by chains as hard to untwine as any of rope or iron.

6

POLITICS

Sentimentality

An old feminist slogan used to say that the personal was the political. Now almost the reverse is true. The political is the personal. Politics is presented as if it is a matter of personalities, and personality is largely a matter of feeling. In the fantasy world of the Cave having the right feelings is what counts. As a consequence, conflict and disagreement are symptoms of bad feeling or ill will. It has come to the point where the Conservative party— by pressure from within—has to demonstrate that it is not the nasty party, instead of coming up with a vision distinct from that of New Labour, or better policies. In the 2005 campaign for the Tory leadership, the buzz word was modernisation. Tone, rather than content, apeing that of New Labour, went an awful long way.

That sentimentality had become a political issue became very clear, if it had not been clear already, with the national outpouring of grief or 'grief' which followed the death of Diana, Princess of Wales. Probably it was indeed grief rather than 'grief'; the feelings were genuine enough, which was more disturbing than if they had been manufactured. Though genuine, they were directed at an image which people had constructed out of their own wish-fulfilment or which had been constructed for them by others in the mass media, rather than at any real person.

Grieving for Diana has by now become such a part of national folklore that it is worth reminding ourselves of the very strange mood of the time. For there were not just the crowds, the flowers and the books of condolence. Nor was there just the pretty unsuppressed hostility towards the House of Windsor in general, and the Queen in particular, for not showing enough grief or for not showing it publicly and demonstrably enough. There was also a vaguely sinister atmosphere in which people who did not share the feelings of the mass—and, as it turned out there were quite a number of refuseniks—felt, or were made to feel, that they should suppress their reservations and pretend to share in the 'national' mood. If fascism is the corporate state from which withdrawal is not possible except by some internal exile of the spirit, there was in that week a fascism of sentiment, kept afloat by the tabloids (though not initiated by them). This fascism of sentiment reached its apogee with Earl Spencer's emotional and undignified speech in the Abbey and the applause which followed that speech first outside and then inside the Abbey.

There was, of course, something beautiful about Diana. Her violent death at so young an age was undeniably tragic. But there was also much symbolic and, in a broad sense, political about her canonisation. It was based on what she stood for and even more on what she was against, as on anything she actually achieved. Rather poignantly, in fact, there has been a rapid evaporation of interest in Diana in the years since her death, not least because she said or did little which was really memorable or extraordinary.

What Diana was against were formality, dignity, emotional restraint, rationalism, and a life led according to the dictates of duty or a strict moral code. It could also be said that she was against hierarchies of various sorts. Her quetioning of hierarchy was evident in her attitude to the arts, for example, (where she favoured the scenes of pop, including pop art, and fashion over those of serious music, painting and literature). In social life much was made of her inclusivity, not that she was afraid to pull rank and bully subordinates when it suited her.

What she was in favour of seemed to derive from her strongly cultivated and not altogether erroneous sense of herself as a victim. So she became the patron of victims— of AIDS, of landmines, of eating disorders, of childhood disease, and in Bosnia, of ethnic cleansing. In some of what she patronised she offered her own emotional rebuke to an establishment which could seem by turns hard-headed and moralistic. In much of this, she was, indeed, proposing her own moralism of sentiment. This new moralism was a handy weapon to deploy against her enemies, who could be represented as unfeeling oppressors, and the same moralism was later deployed by Diana's supporters, including the Prime Minister, against her critics.

As an example of her own moralism, Diana complained about her mother-in-law calling the shots, without any apparent recognition of her mother-in-law's role as the Queen. Her emotionalistic moralism also licensed her New Age consultations of alternative therapists and fortune tellers, as well as her own self-exposure in the Andrew Morton book and the Panorama interview, as if, again in the spirit of the age, she was engaging in some process of healing through public confessional.

One may ask why personal sentimentality of the Diana variety is political. It is political because with it go along a whole raft of attitudes and policies which are political in the narrow as well as the broad sense. It should be obvious that AIDS is a highly political cause, combining aggressive 'non-judgementalism' on sexual matters with complaints about third world poverty and the profits of drugs companies, but let us consider the apparently less controversial cases of landmines and ethnic cleansing.

I do not doubt that most people of goodwill would deplore the use of landmines. They would also unite in condemning the impulses which lead to ethnic cleansing and the practical results of ethnic cleansing. Sentiment would, then, line us up against both. But is sentiment enough in politics? May it not bring with it illusions as dangerous as the very features of the world it would condemn? What does the sentimentalist do when confronted by an evil will or by an irresolvable dispute? The problem is that the sentimentalist, in seeing the world only in her terms, is constitutionally unready to admit the existence of either of radical evil or of a genuinely irresolvable dispute.

Landmines are horrible in their effects, which include the blowing up of children even after whatever conflict they have been used in has died down. But does that mean that we should ban them worldwide or that we should be persuaded by pictures of limbless landmine victims to outlaw their use completely? We would seem thereby to be ruling out in advance what might on occasion be the case, that only landmines might afford a small or weak nation any measure of defence against a vicious, powerful aggressor.

Secondly, let us take ethnic cleansing. This is something we would no doubt prefer did not happen, but wishing something does not make it so. It is not clear that there are not situations in the world, even now, where neighbouring and overlapping populations are simply unable to co-exist peacefully. We, from our position of multicultural sentimentality, might not even begin to understand how people could come to be in such a mind-set. But given that such a mind-set is actually by no means unknown (even in one region of the United Kingdom), it is not clear that some measure of semi-spontaneous ethnic cleansing might not prove at least a temporary respite for the populations concerned. This appears to have happened in Londonderry, a few decades ago a major centre of inter-communal violence, but which in contrast to Belfast in more recent times was so no longer. Nor, the barbarities of the Serbs notwithstanding, is it all clear that backing the Kosovan Albanians has done much more than put the boot on the other foot, with churches now being burned rather than mosques. Maybe in this case too a separation of the peoples might be the best outcome, and one which, under the KLA seems to be happening anyway.

Whatever might be said about ethnic cleansing itself—and I have taken the example only because it is about as unpopular a cause as could be found in the modern world, accompanied as it usually is by atrocities—the fundamental objection to the politics of sentimentality is that it is unable to conceive of a situation in which people might come to think that landmines or ethnic cleansing might be the least bad solution to their predicament. It is, in fact, sentimental to think that there is no problem which cannot be solved, given a modicum of goodwill on both sides, and dangerously sentimental to think that reason and compassion or, worse, compassion on its own are a match for evil. The goodwill may not be there, and being smiled at by Princess Diana or being lectured on conflict resolution by Presidents Carter or Clinton may not be enough to produce it.

For people who are comfortably off and who care about nothing beyond the present—inhabitants of the fantasy world of the Cave, in other words,—it can be very hard to imagine how others might find something worth fighting for, even transcending good will. Sentimentality can at times make one blind to some very real and not necessarily negative human passions and loyalties. 'Caring' on the sentimental, Diana mode, can be little more than a cover for the insensitivity of telling others that what they really care about is worth nothing, and best quietly forgotten. This is itself a form of intellectual or emotional imperialism, though one in which many of us unthinkingly engage, and which makes it all but impossible for most of us to have any real understanding of situations of conflict, such as those in Ireland or the Balkans. We just have neither the means nor the sympathy to understand the passions and commitments at stake.

But it is not only in conflicts abroad that we are confronted with a politics of sentiment. Most of us will still remember the tide of elation which gripped the country in May 1997, when New Labour won its first election victory. Significantly this was only a few months before the even greater tide of mourning which followed the death of Diana, and it is surely not coincidental that Tony Blair himself—a self-confessed emotionalist— seemed to be orchestrating the mood of the whole country on both occasions. It was, of course, Blair who used the phrase 'the People's Princess' on the morning of Diana's death, and who, rather than the Queen or the Royal Family, presided over the events which unravelled that week, including producing an unbearably hammy reading of *Corinthians* 1.13 at the funeral service itself. Never mind that even in 1997, some nine million people had actually had the insensitivity to vote for the despised Conservatives. On that May morning in 1997, it appeared that everyone believed, to use one of Labour's slogans, that 'things could only get better'.

That things could *only* get better was not a rational belief. There were, to be sure, plenty of ways in which things could have got better. We all knew that transport, education, health and welfare were in a poor state after (or even after) 17 years of Tory rule. But in May 1997 it was hard to see that New Labour had any policies which would actually improve any of these things, and more than eight years and two parliaments on, when if anything things have only got worse, it is even harder. It was indeed notable that for the first couple of years Labour covered gaps and inadequacies in its policies by blaming 'the previous government', but after a while this excuse became less and less credible. Now, apart from putting more and more money into the very same 'public services' which were responsible for many of the problems in the first place, and with then smothering them with oppressive management and meaningless if not mendacious 'targets', it is unclear that the government has any policies at all.

But policies were not really the issue in 1997. Then it was a triumph, if not of the will, at least of sentiment. Things were bound to get better because we had a government which was not composed of weird and sleazy Tories. Nor was it Socialist either. What it was was the Third Way. The Third Way is nothing less than a utopian amalgam of the caring bits of socialism with the efficient bits of capitalism, individualism with community, community with individual freedom, the market without its failures and the welfare state without its built in inefficiencies and welfare dependency.

It was, in fact, pure fantasy. It was sentimental in that it involved a belief that you could reconcile opposites, providing only good will, and that everyone's aims could be reconciled to everyone's satisfaction. Logically, of course, the Third Way is a non-starter, which is why I refer to it as utopian. In common with other utopian visions it pretends that the contradictions of conflicting political ideals are not really contradictions. It pretends that you can have universal liberty without compromising equality (or vice versa); that welfarism can be promulgated without state control, ever-increasing regulation and the demoralisation of those who come to depend on and manipulate the welfare system; that equality of opportunity (for all) will not inevitably mean the denial for some of what their efforts, talent and upbringing have merited for them; and, most recently, that untrammelled civil liberties and human rights are consistent with security.

One can pursue one of the contradictory ideals perfectly logically, and one can also attempt to work out how, in given circumstances, to modify one or other of the conflicting ideals to fit in to an overall policy in which none of the ideals is realised in its pure, unsullied state. But what one cannot do is to pretend that the contradictions are not there. This purely logical difficulty will exist even were there not the usual messy empirical constraints on the realisation of political programmes, such as finiteness of resources, inequalities of ability and effort, and the perennial tendency of rulers and bureaucrats to feather their own nests.

But, against both logic and experience, the Third Way was an effort to have politics without disagreement and conflict; and not surprisingly it degenerated fairly quickly into a politics without substance. Nor was it surprising that one of the first problems for this politics of sentimentality arose in Ulster. In Ulster still (even after numerous pledges by the IRA to renounce violence) there really are people in significant numbers whose conflicting ambitions and principles really cannot be reconciled, and who indeed, violence aside, both have intelligible and honorable positions. The problem is that these positions are irreconcilable, and any lasting settlement will inevitably mean the abandonment of some long held ambitions, at least on one side.

This was not a good place for Third Wayism, which would almost inevitably succeed in conveying to one side (or both) that really 'we', the rulers from over the water, don't actually take your aims and ideals seriously. In 1997 Mo Mowlam, an egregious exponent of the politics of sentimentality, was initially put in charge. Hardly surprisingly, on her death in 2005, she was immediately canonised as 'The People's Politician' for her touchy-feelyness and her 'unconventional' manner (just as Diana was the People's Princess and Jill Dando, the murdered television personality, the People's Presenter). What Mo Mowlam actually achieved in Ulster is, though, far harder to determine, for when she left office the Good Friday agreement appeared beset by endless wrangles and problems.

In fairness to Dr Mowlam, though, who in herself showed some personal courage in Northern Ireland, her immediate successors did little better, if only because, Tony Blair's emoting on the subject notwithstanding, the Good Friday agreement was either never an agreement at all, or one on which no one is agreed about what was actually supposed to be agreed, or both. Eight years after the Good Friday agreement—which was supposed to unite all people of good will in Ulster into the political middle ground—the only political runners with any real support are Sinn Fein/IRA and Dr Paisley's DUP. This is presumably not what the framers of the Good Friday agreement had in mind.

Whether real progress has actually been made over the IRA's 2005 declaration that the bullet has been abandoned very much remains to be seen. Controversy also attends the motivation for their laying down of arms (if such it is). Is it because of a genuine change of heart away from the bullet towards the ballot box? Is it because they began to realise that they might do well at the ballot box, and the withdrawal from violence merely tactical and possibly temporary? Or is it because (as some think) by the mid-1990s the IRA had in fact been very largely defeated militarily, or had at least been ground down into stalemate by the security services?

The one thing we should have learned from the history of Ireland over the last century is that wishing something does not make it so, and also that since the 1920s the IRA (and its off-shoots) have been masters of the manipulation of wish and sentiment. Peace in Ulster may be achieved, but only by first making it impossible for the propagators of violence on both sides to operate, and that will not be achieved by good will alone.

Third Wayism is sentimental because it amounts to a hope, well intentioned maybe, that in politics differences can always be resolved and conflicts avoided (in contrast to Mrs Thatcher, say, whose politics thrived on conflict and on facing opponents down). It is sentimental also because it is in effect denying the existence of real conflict, and also of real maliciousness. And it is a dangerous illusion for just that reason.

Nothing could be more foreign to the spirit of our time and to the sentimentality of Third Wayism than the remarkable painting by El Greco exhibited recently in London under the title *The Adoration of the Name of Jesus*. The Holy Name of Jesus is indeed being venerated in the painting, but what is actually being celebrated is the Battle of Lepanto of 1571. The Pope, King Philip II of Spain and the Doge of Venice are all kneeling, giving thanks for Christianity's victory over the Turkish fleet and the forces of Islam. This was a decisive victory as it turned out, after several centuries of religious and military threat from the East (even if the Turks still had to be turned back from the gates of Vienna in 1683 and were not expelled from Budapest until 1686).

All the history of the extraordinary rise of Islam and its eventual partial reverse, and the spirit behind it, which seemed so significant at the time, is wholly alien to the spirit of our age. It is nowhere taught to children in our schools. Maybe because of our ignorance and forgetfulness of our past, it may be that what Islam failed to do by military might four centuries ago, it is starting to do by immigration, so much so that there is an amazing prediction that Holland is set to have a Muslim majority sometime this century. Whether this piece of demographical projection has any basis beyond the purely statistical, I do not know. What is clear is that there are areas in many western European cities, such as Rotterdam and Bradford, with concentrations of Muslims who show little inclination to integrate with the host society. There have strong suspicions that some of the insurgency in Iraq has been organised from within the immigrant community in Oslo. Oslo! About as far from any traditional centre of Islamic practice as one could imagine. From our own country, already young men travel abroad to fight on the side of our enemies and against our own troops, or to return here to plant bombs on public transport.

We are only just beginning to wake up to the implications of any of this. For all of our good intentions and sentimentality, there are people in the world, who would like to bring down us and our way of life. Some of them are in our own country, fellow-countrymen of ours, willing to use the cowardly weapon of suicide bombing in London itself, or even more cowardly to urge and organise others to do so. In our sentimentality, we haven't a clue what to do, other than wait for the next terrorist outrage. The threat is not in the conventional sense military, and the methods of 1571 would not work, even were they acceptable.

Meanwhile, those who would destroy our freedoms and even our lives regard us with contempt, not just for our sentimentality, but also for our obsessions with the dregs of celebrity, with drugs and with the trivia of the mass media, to say nothing of our feeble attitudes to education, to self-discipline and to personal relationships. It may be that suicide bombers are motivated not by any rational cause, but are like the Baader-Meinhof and Red Brigade terrorists of the 1970s simply looking for occasions to justify their adolescent murderous destructiveness; nevertheless certain powerful strains of Islam, in their appeal to the resentment of the 'humiliated', do provide a ready vehicle for such destructiveness, just as anarchist Marxism did in the earlier instances. However not everything that Islam says about the decadence of the West or understands about our sentimentality and moral weakness is wrong, and we need to appreciate that too.

But sentimental politics does not just fatally weaken

those in its thrall. It has its own distinctly sinister aspect. Although proponents of the Third Way, if any still exist, do not like to be reminded of the fact, New Labour is not the first time that the idea of a non-divisive and all-inclusive politics has been tried. Reconciliation of the political opposites of socialism and capitalism, and of the interests of bosses and workers and of all other sections of society was precisely the ideology of Sir Oswald Mosley's New Party in the 1930s. There too there would be an ill-inclusive political big tent in which all different interests would participate and be united. And Mosley, in turn, derived his Third Wayism from Mussolini's Italy.

Modern politics, as represented by New Labour, is not Mussolini's fascism. There has in Britain—at least since the 1970s—been no undercurrent of violence in or near mainstream politics. There have been no bully boys or private armies needing to be 'controlled' by the seizure of power of those who actually set them up. But, then, in our fantasy world, one would not expect there to be, for our fantasies demand and sustain a post-modern form of power in which the subjects are perfectly content with their lethargy and slumber.

We should, though, note the pretension of New Labour to be the People's Party, as if in a pluralist society there could be such a thing, and as if—what is manifestly not the case—there were a single vision of the good life uniting the whole population. Some might think, that in the face of all logic and experience, it might be nice if there were; that is where the sentimentality comes in. But what happens when the leaders actually start believing such a thing, very likely sincerely? That is when the politics of sentimentality begins to look rather less innocuous. But it explains not just the exasperation evinced by Blair and the Blairites towards those who disagree with them—for how could anyone of good feeling and decent intentions fail to agree with them, or even more, cast any doubt on the government's benevolence, including their costly benevolence towards the people of Iraq?

A basis in sentiment rather than in reason or political reality also explains the government's increasingly technocratic, authoritarian and extra-parliamentary tendencies. For, on the sentimental view, where we are all united on ends, all that is left for politics to do is to 'deliver' what we all agree we want. Parliament becomes on this view at best irrelevant and at worst positively obstructive. So avoid it as far as possible, and take out the awkward bits, such as the unreformed House of Lords (and no doubt, in due course, the judges). And authoritarian because sentimentality cannot tolerate the challenging of sentiment and the untidiness of dissent— which can be explained only by malice on the part of the dissenters. They, as we all know, are in one way or another 'the forces of conservatism', whether they be old style trade unionists, hereditary peers, civil libertarians or— worst of all—traditional Tories.

'To every nation a purpose. To every party a cause. And now, at last, Party and nation joined in the same cause for the same purpose: to set our people free.' Thus Tony Blair at the 1999 Labour Party conference.

It is unsettling to hear that a nation has a purpose—rather than being a community without purpose itself, but within which many different purposes could be worked out by many different institutions, agencies and people. It is also deeply sentimental, based as it is on the erroneous belief that a nation could be an organism of that sort, united in feeling and purpose, except during some very temporary war-time threat to its very existence. In his 1995 speech to the Labour Party conference Blair spoke of 'a new spirit in the nation based on working together, unity, solidarity, partnership. One Britain. That is the patriotism of the future. Where never again do we fight our politics by appealing to one section of the nation at the expense of the other.' And when in power things do not work out quite like that, and one does have to appeal to one section of the nation at the expense of the other, those appealed against have, by all the political powers and presentational skills one has, to be marginalized. They must not be allowed to destroy the fantasy of unity and modernity.

The worry about the politics of sentimentality is not that its adherents—whether Tony Blair or Princess Diana or whoever—are not sincere. The worry is precisely that they are sincere. Their sincerity is one which leads not only to the denial of real problems and to the closing of one's eyes to deep conflict, even when such conflict threatens us. It also leads, unforgivably, to the demonisation of opponents. For in an all-inclusive third way politics, in which all decent people are by definition assembled in a big tent, those outside the tent are, equally by definition, either incorrigibly stupid or incorrigibly wicked.

There is no longer, in the politics of sentimentality, any room for honest disagreement among honest opponents: only 'issues' which can be 'addressed' by the patronising techniques of 'conflict resolution'. Where these techniques fail, we are, in the modern demonology, left only with the irredeemable outcasts of our time, the forces of conservatism, Ulster protestants, Serbs, Israeli right-wingers, Muslim terrorists, American fundamentalists—all those awkward enough to have commitments standing in the way of the agenda of sentimentality.

That, up to a point, Third Wayism is becoming unstuck over Iraq is not surprising. Tony Blair appeared quite genuinely not to believe that reasonable people would not agree with him in wanting to get rid of the unreasonable Saddam Hussein and in wanting to set up a 'big tent' in Iraq. In this he not only displayed the assumption common to sentimentalists that to those inspired by (good) moral fervour, violence can be justified. He also showed himself initially strongly in the grip of the sentimental assumption that there can be no real disagreements between reasonable people, and that those who disagree—dissidents—are by their very nature unreasonable. And finally, on Iraq itself, like many sentimentalists who ignore the history which makes people what they are and the way in which 'reasonableness' is always rooted in the historical experience of a people, Blair appeared to believe that our democratic institutions could simply be transplanted, *sans phrase*, on to Iraqi soil.

All this has, of course, unravelled, both in Britain and in Iraq. This is not to say that the war may not have been a good thing, but the contentiousness of the war has certainly shown that Tony Blair himself can no longer pretend to incarnate all sweetness and light in the British body politic. This, as far as it goes, is a good thing.

It is also a good thing that the British public is, by now, thoroughly fed up with the bullying of both opponents and supporters with which the Blairite project has been marked. They are fed up too by its rampant cronyism, the rewarding and ennoblement of supporters on a scale as great as any other government, despite New Labour's promise to be cleaner than clean in this respect. They are fed up too with the deceit of the government, over matters as various as Iraq, Railtrack, the Foot and Mouth crisis, the Mittal affair, and much else besides (all amply documented in Peter Oborne's book *The Rise of Political Lying*, London, 2005). They are fed up, too, by what appears to be the ultimate Blairite arrogance, that if the cause is right all these little things (deceit, cronyism, etc) can be, should be excused by all whose hearts (!) are in the right place. But that, of course, takes us back to the politics of sentimentality: that good feeling and belief in the rightness of one's cause justify cutting corners, particularly where those corners are occupied by unpleasant people unconvinced of our goodness of heart.

Widespread disillusion with Blairism notwithstanding, what is far less clear is that the British public has taken to heart the more fundamental lesson that domestic politics is just as riven and contradictory as foreign policy. For the New Labour promises of caring capitalism, of a huge welfare system which does not diminish enterprise, and of universal equality of opportunity without diminution of liberty and of reward are just as chimerical and utopian in 2005 as they were in 1997. Many of those who had become opposed to New Labour, in the 2005 election supported the Liberal Democrats, whose ideas are in these crucial respects very close to Labour's. Even more striking the Tories, who may deep down have some scepticism on some of these matters, chose to run an election campaign which challenged none of the chimeras at a fundamental level. None of this gives any confidence that the policy of the sentimental reconciliation of opposites which we see incarnated in New Labour will be significantly challenged by any political party in the near future.

A deeply worrying, though entirely predictable manifestation of the fact that the politics of sentimentality still rules the roost is the whole farrago of the Live8 concert and the Make Poverty History campaign. We defined the politics of sentimentality as a form of politics in which feeling is all and doing means nothing. These campaigns are not even collecting money from their supporters. Their supporters are supposed simply to show that, in their millions, they care, mainly by going to a free rock concert, wearing white wrist bands and shouting insults and obscenities at politicians. How any of this is supposed to help starving Africans is entirely obscure, though no doubt it makes those involved feel good.

Any actual doing is left to the hapless politicians. For once, one might evince some sympathy for politicians, were it not that, following on from Bob Geldof's earlier knighthood, they once more cravenly sucked up to the very people who were insulting them. For the doing is far more difficult that the absurdly simply nostrums of the campaigners would have it, with their ritual denunciations of age old colonial sins and modern free trade.

Few are those brave enough to point out that aid and reparations for ancestral sins will do little more than scratch the surface of the problems of Africa. Reparations and debt-cancellation will do nothing permanently to improve the lot of today's victims of yesterday's oppressions—unless those same victims are then able to themselves to lift themselves out of their predicament by their own on-going efforts. In addition debt cancellation may have only the effect of reducing credit-worthiness even further. Aid, which looks good on paper, is often tied to the purchase of goods from Western companies.

In any case, assistance from outside will continue to be unavailing if it leads only to a situation in which more such assistance is needed once the first tranche is used up. Ultimately the best, and only way for poor countries to improve the lot of their peoples is to develop their own economies themselves, through free trade. Free trade, in releasing human enterprise and capital is the most efficient way so far discovered for a people permanently to better themselves, as belatedly China and even more significantly India are discovering. So, unless one is saying that there is something significantly different about Africans, why not in Africa too?

But sentimentalists do not like free trade, because free trade involves hard work and, while undoubtedly raising the lot of all who participate, inevitably also produces inequalities. And the means to produce free trade involve detailed and doubtless protracted negotiations over years. Far easier to live in the world of fantasy. Like Sir Bob's followers, parade one's own virtue and caring in a cost-free manner, and blame politicians, financiers and the 'system' in what is a classic case of the politics of sentimentality.

7

EDUCATION

Fantasies

We are governed by a politics of sentimentality. We should not, then, be surprised to discover that there is also an educational world equally ruled by sentimental fantasy. The Cave is a progenitor of illusions which flatter the subject, and which, like a drug or the experience machine, give him or her a sense of achievement without the effort or the struggle or the ability necessary to produce it in reality.

Modern educational fantasies derive from two sources. Though different in style and inspiration, these sources agree on one crucial point, which, very simply, is just the most important point of all. Both conspire to deny that the primary, if not the only purpose of education, is the removal of ignorance. This involves the transmission to those who do not know these things of the best that has been thought and known.

One of the sources of modern educational thinking is the child-centred philosophy of early romanticism, as represented by Rousseau. Education should allow the child to develop naturally and to fulfil his or her own potential—whatever his or her nature and whatever he or she has potential for. There is no sense here of original sin, no inkling that in most of our natures there are negative as well as positive impulses. Nor is there any recognition of the way civilised life not only builds on, but also corrects nature. There is no recognition that education is, by its nature, a matter of acquainting strangers to the human condition with the voices and conversations of mankind. These voices and conversations which do not come naturally. They need to be painstakingly taught and learned.

Educational child-centeredness undermines the authority of the teacher, and even the need for a teacher altogether. The child, it is believed, will discover what is needed for him or herself, in play, in encounters with nature. There is no need for formal instruction in things which are at best irrelevant and often harmful to boot in that they represent the elitist lumber of the past. In the fantasy world of education elite is a term of abuse, as it implies unnatural gradations of class and status.

For different reasons, many of the same conclusions will be drawn from the equally fantastic vision of education which derives indirectly from elements of the pragmatism of the philosopher John Dewey and directly from its application by his followers to education. On this view, education should be focused on practical skills and the solving of actual problems in real life. Real education must always start from some real life experience of the child, and a problem which arises from that, on, say, how a substance like rubber is handled and used in some practical context (such as car tyres). In addressing this problem, we might make enquiries into a lot of traditional subjects, such as chemistry, geography, history, politics and technology. But their value and the value of the whole process will depend on the efficacy of the solutions ultimately arrived at, again in real-life contexts. In this view traditional subjects are artificial abstractions from real life and its problems and experiences.

A crucial aspect of this Deweyesque, instrumentalist view of education is that education is primarily an exercise in communal problem-solving. All should co-operate on equal terms, pupils and teachers alike, and which admits of no ready-made solutions. As in the romantic vision, education is a matter of discovery about real-life matters and concerns, and the teacher ultimately has no more authority than the pupils. The teacher is a facilitator rather than a source of knowledge, and the educational process is an exercise in democratically structured problem-solving. Education thus models democracy in miniature, and, as with the romantics, it should not be conceived as a process of (uselessly) acquiring worn out knowledge or imbibing the prejudices of the elites of the past.

In both of these visions, we must take care not to undermine the self-esteem of the pupil. This is no way out opinion in today's educational world. Sir Christopher Ball, former Warden of Keble College Oxford and now

Chancellor of the University of Derby, and member of countless governmental and other advisory bodies on education, maintains that low self esteem and lack of confidence in the learner is the most important reason why people fail to learn, while high achievers have boundless self-esteem and confidence. (Pascal? Socrates? Coleridge? Darwin? Bruckner? Elgar? Kafka?) The other reasons, and the only other reasons, according to Sir Christopher are weak motivation, insufficient ability and lack of opportunity. Significantly there is no mention of poor teaching of the basics or insufficiently demanding content as contributing to poor learning. The main job for 'educators' (not teachers, note) is to build up people's self-esteem and to help them to strengthen their own motivation; and, according to Sir Christopher, when an imposed curriculum replaces choice and 'exploratory learning', motivation will decline as resistance to learning increases.[7]

In referring to self-esteem Sir Christopher touches on one of the idols of the age. In pop psychological parlance we hear of so many people, from school children and members of ethnic minorities right up to the highest of celebrities and even members of the royal family lacking in self-esteem. Lack of self-esteem is said to be personally and psychologically crippling. And in order to cope with it, people are counselled to lower their sights.

In some cases, this might be right. Maybe I should not feel a loss of self-esteem just because I cannot ski off piste (an arena for a happy few) or prove Goldbach's conjecture (which no one can). Maybe for a person of pretty average ambition and accomplishment, some self-esteem is due for being able to ski moderately competently on piste and for being able to understand what Goldbach's conjecture is and why its proof is problematic. There are people who do themselves down and think the less of themselves for bad reasons.

But simply lowering one's sights in this way cannot be a general answer to loss of self-esteem. There are certain things any self-respecting person ought to be able to do, and certain ways they should behave. They should do their best to reach these standards. Teachers particularly, and all who are involved in the education and upbringing of the young, have a duty to point this out to those in their care. If self-esteem is secured through laziness or evasion of problems or through a cosy self-deception about what is really required, it may actually be a far less desirable state than its opposite, which might encourage us to do as well as we should.

Not only that, but in education and throughout life, the best way to achieve solid self esteem is to overcome a weakness or obstacle. In many cases telling someone that a weakness is not really a weakness or, as with so many teachers, failing to point out and correct mistakes and sloppiness is not just patronising. It is also the cruellest thing we can do. It deprives the person concerned of the chance of the real self-esteem which comes from overcoming and self-overcoming.

It follows then that most of what is done in classrooms

and elsewhere to protect damage to self-esteem is actually a way of ensuring that people never actually achieve self-esteem of a worthwhile sort. Far from being the kindest and most positive thing which can be done, as Sir Christopher apparently believes, stripping people of discomfort at lack of achievement can be the unkindest. As Nietzsche put it in *The Gay Science* (section 338) in pitying us and removing difficulties from our path, 'our 'benefactors' diminish our worth and our will more than our enemies do.'

When tests were first introduced for seven year old pupils in state primary schools, my son was in the first cohort to be tested. There was a great amount of talk at the time against the very principle of testing children so young, and of the damage this would do to their self-esteem.

Far less damage, I reflected, than if they were not tested and not rigorously taught. If children cannot read adequately at the age of 7, they have an educational deficit which becomes increasingly hard to compensate for, and which may well be the root cause of much pupil dissatisfaction in secondary schools. If a school is not teaching the vast majority of its pupils to read by the age of 7, serious questions need to be asked about it and its teachers. Even in their imperfect state, it was just this that the seven year old tests were designed to reveal, over and above individual attainment.

Yet at the meeting at my son's school at which parents were being told about the tests, what the parents seemed most interested in was whether their children would be 'stressed' by them. They were not interested in the nature or point of the tests, despite their huge importance both for the pupils individually and for the school as a whole. The teachers spent most of the time assuring the parents that the children would not be stressed, and even that they would not really notice they were being tested.

The whole tenor of the discussion on the part of both parents and teachers was that nothing must be done to shake the fragile self-esteem of the pupils, whatever the long-term consequences. In our treatment of ourselves, and of our children particularly, we are more indulgent and sentimental than any previous generation. Yet, paradoxically it seems, we also hear that our children are more stressed and lacking in self-esteem than any previous generation.

But is this really a paradox? The more indulgent we are to our children—as exemplified by the incident of the reading tests—and the more we keep them insulated from challenge and difficulty, the less they will be prepared for challenge and difficulty when, as they inevitably will, they appear. The less they will be able to overcome them, and the more stressed and self-doubting they will be.

This is just what we see with many young people today. Because of our fears about damaging their self-esteem, we remove from them the occasions in which they might learn academically and also develop the virtues of hard work, application and self-reliance.

Lacking self-reliance and self-motivation, they are bored. And when the stream of television and other essentially passive electronic life supports systems fail to engage, they turn to drink and drugs.

This is what will be seen in any town centre any weekend evening. Often enough the young will complain that there is 'nothing to do around here'. It doesn't seem to occur to them that they might do some things for themselves. Someone else is supposed to entertain them. But having given them an education in which, in the name of self-esteem, the opportunities for self-reliance and self-motivation are diminished to virtually zero, should one be surprised?

Self esteem, then, rather than the transmission of some hard intellectual heritage becomes the paramount theme in education. For, according to the romantics, what we are about is fostering the blossoming of the child's existing personality. According to the pragmatists, every contribution to solving a problem has a value. If it is a real problem, rather than something factitiously got up by a teacher or an examining board, everyone will have a worthwhile perspective or view on it. From both points of view, the worst thing we could do would be to crush the learner's spirit by correcting or criticising his or her contribution. In our efforts to avoid this, and also to avoid the indoctrinatory imposition of past intellectual baggage, we will systematically diminish the status of the teacher. From being a person with intellectual authority, we will degrade him or her to being no more than a manager or facilitator.

These visions and their converging outcomes are fantasies. They are fantasies because they deny certain obvious facts, such as differences of potential among pupils and the inherent potential for laziness, malice and other negative traits we all share and which we have overcome by curbing some of our natural tendencies. They also completely overlook the extent to which our lives and very identities are formed by cultural influences and forms, which we can learn only by being taught. Furthermore problem solving, even at its most immediately practical, will be much easier—to say the least—if we know (or are taught) the things mankind as a whole has taken generations to discover. And this is to say nothing of the value of the arts and sciences beyond the narrowly practical, knowledge of which greatly enhances the lives of all who learn about them, and also the societies in which they are practiced.

Education, then, is not primarily a process of the self-revelation of a character I already have. To think in this romantic way overlooks the extent to which character is substantially formed in and through cultural encounters, including formal education. Nor is it a matter of the acquisition of content free 'transferable' skills. Most high level skills are not transferable from one area or subject matter to another, but are specific to specific fields, such as physics or football or music, and are not in any case independent of a surrounding context of knowledge.

Nor is education a matter of democratic problem solving or of democracy in miniature. Not all problems are best solved in a democratic group, nor is learning to be conceived in terms of political processes. Education is actually a structured activity of initiation of those initially ignorant of them into existing and worthwhile forms of knowledge and experience. In this activity, there are inevitably clear distinctions between teachers and pupils, between achievements of greater and lesser quality, between answers which are good and those which are less good, and between different areas of knowledge and experience each of which has through human experience and endeavour developed its own logic and methods and each of which has initially to be learned on its own terms. In all of this there is no substitute for intellectual aptitude and hard work, nor can the authority of one who knows more be gain-said. This may all be discomforting to the 'self-esteem' of pupils, individually and collectively, and also to a government of fantasists intent of recognising the 'achievements' of all.

One should not, of course, be persuaded that the fantasists in charge of education are entirely disinterested in their efforts to recognise the achievements of all. Whether they are politicians, bureaucrats or teachers, all have a vested interest in showing that standards are 'rising', and few are honest enough or brave enough to admit that there is a great deception going on with exams and standards. This explains is why remarks of the sort I am about to make will not be answered with any real attempt to examine educational standards. Instead, I will be accused of being an elitist, denigrating the 'successes' of our young people. One despairs.

It is precisely a fantasy—of continually rising standards and ever more inclusive achievement—which has been driving educational policy for two decades or more. As is well known, in Britain and elsewhere since the 1960s there has been a constant drive to have all children, from the ages of 5 right up to 16 and even beyond, in the same schools. All differences of talent, motivation and background are to be ignored in a pretence that all children are the same and should be treated the same. Discrimination by ability is not allowed in the schools of the Cave, and is called—as a term of abuse—elitist.

Following the widespread introduction of comprehensive schooling we now have comprehensive exams, whose main characteristic is that no one must fail. Such indeed was the very reason for the introduction of the GCSE in 1988, an exam intended for all pupils reaching the end of compulsory schooling at the age of 16. Before that there was a two tier system, of academic exams for some and of more vocationally oriented tests for the rest.

To egalitarians this was objectionable in itself, and also, even with the two tier system, too many 16 year olds left school with no awards at all. The GCSE was to be an examination for all, as the slogan had it, and one which all would pass in some shape or form. One could not having nothing but support for a genuine attempt to raise the educational ambitions of the less academic, nor for raising their levels of achievement, but the GCSE has done neither of those things.

GCSE was first taken in 1988. Between then and 2003 the pass rate increased by 46%, and the number of awards in the top two grades has risen by 145%. In 2005, 650,000 pupils took 5.7 million papers, of which 97.6% were graded as passes of some sort.

A triumph? Not really, if one looks at the finer detail. In matters of school exams, even when one fantasises, reality has a nasty habit of kicking in. Although a grade G in the GCSE is reckoned officially to be a pass, in practice only grade C and above is really rated by anyone. Here the position is much less satisfying to the illusionists of the Cave. Over 40% of the results were below grade C, and in maths it was 50%. Moreover, 30,000 pupils left school in 2003 without even 1 GCSE pass. Not, of course, that anyone acquainted with young people and without a vested interest in maintaining the illusion really believes that pupils are 46% or 145% better educated than they were 18 years ago.

However, for the illusionists even the GCSE is not enough. Because there are still pupils who get poor grades or even no grades at all, the exam itself has to be swept away, to be replaced by an over arching diploma which, it seems, no one will fail and in which all 'achievement' and all manner of achievement will be 'recognised'. The thought that the GCSE exam is already too easy, and that those who fail deserve to fail is no longer thinkable in educational circles. According to the government's own discussion document on the reform of the exam system ('14-19: Opportunity and Excellence', January 2003) failure and difficulty in the GCSE is too demotivating to pupils. What we need, apparently, is yet another reform of the exam system which will ensure that no one leaves school without a qualification, and in a somewhat crab-wise direction an official pat on the head for everyone appears to be the direction in which educational policy is moving.

If the GCSE improvement is not credible, even less is that at A level, the exam pupils take at the age of 18. Over the past 23 years, every year, A level grades have 'improved'. In 1982 8.6% of A levels were at grade A (the highest grade). In 1989 (when the Secretary of State took over control of public examinations) it was 11.4%. In 2005 was a staggering 22.8%. Anyone daring to express reservations about this is dismissed as a perpetual carper or, even worse, an elitist. We should be 'celebrating' the achievements of our young people and those of their teachers, who, according to the illusionists of the Cave, are the best they have ever been.

Various uncomfortable facts are simply ignored—

such as serious grade erosion in maths, a grade E in 1988 being worth a B in 2004, according to an authoritative study by the Curriculum, Evaluation and Management Centre of University of Durham; or the fact that it is now possible to do an A level in French without any study of classical French literature; or the removal of the prose translation from Latin A level; or the fact that, despite the massive expansion of the system overall, the number of those taking physics has more than halved since 1984, while chemistry entries have fallen by a third and maths by more than a quarter; or, in more general terms, the extremely low level of knowledge and learning of most young people today. Surveys continually reveal astonishing ignorance among the young about the Second World War and Auschwitz, and this despite an obsessive concentration in GCSE and A level history on the Nazis and the Holocaust.

None of this is the fault of the young people themselves, who in many cases seem keen to work. It is the fault of the education system of the Cave which keeps them in ignorance, and which we are commanded to cheer.

Nowhere do we see the operation of fantasy in the educational world more clearly than in higher education. Before 1992, around a fifth of young people went to universities and polytechnics to do degrees, and most of them got them. The upshot was that Britain had as many graduates per head of the population as any comparable society, and a great deal more than many of our competitors in Europe. But to have a qualification which only a fifth can get is inherently elitist, and even worse, within the group with degrees, the middle classes were far more heavily represented than the traditional working classes. Never mind that among middle classes just are those groups where academic learning is both valued and mandatory, or that many from the former working classes earn as much or more than such typical representatives of the middle classes as teachers, middle managers, public services administrators and officials, and even university professors. The mere fact of something which looks better than other things is offensive.

So, at a stroke, in 1992 the number of universities was doubled, by the simple and wonderfully cost-free device of calling the former polytechnics universities. At the same time the number of students was also doubled, by forcing all universities, old and new, to take more and more students. Now the participation rate is 43% and the government is insistent it has to be 50% by 2010.

Of course, a status or qualification which was valuable because of its scarcity will not still be valuable when it is held by half the population. But perhaps that is part of the point, to erode a distinction of quality. At any rate no one can now pretend that university education is about quality, as opposed to quantity. It is not as if there are hordes of well qualified and well educated young people queuing up to read hard subjects like maths and physics. Thanks in many cases to poor teaching in these areas, over the past fifteen years there have been catastrophic declines in the numbers of people doing maths and physics at A level, as we have seen, even despite erosion of content in the syllabuses. Universities simply cannot fill their places in maths and the sciences, and the slack is taken up in courses of uncertain quality: in business, media studies, sports science, any amount of social work and nursing courses, and a host of new and hitherto unknown disciplines such as aromatherapy, golf course studies, peace studies, tourism and leisure, to say nothing of animation, caring services and recreational management.

But instead of coming to terms with the implications of a disastrous expansion of so-called higher education, or with any realistic moves to improve the school education it provides in state schools, the government throws the whole weight of its might into a campaign against Oxford and Cambridge and other elite universities for not admitting enough ill-prepared students from state schools. This campaign is backed by financial penalties for universities which fail to meet government monitored targets on admissions, and by a new bureaucratic department dedicated to its implementation. In all but name, top universities now have to accept quotas of students from the poorest schools, whether they are adequately prepared for university work or not.

Unfortunately, either out of pragmatism or out of

ideology, too many of these universities are all too ready
to implement these policies, whose effect is to discrimi-
nate against the hard working and the well educated. In
all but name we in Britain now have a quota system in
our universities. And the effect of such a system cannot
but impact on the quality of the teaching and the
standards of degrees themselves, for both will have to be
adapted to deal with the new type of intake (and one can
just imagine the official opprobrium which will attach to
any department or faculty which fails too many of its all-
inclusive clintele). The irony is that this happening here
just at a time when many American states are moving
away from positive discrimination. California, for
example, has recently declared any such policy illegal after
a disastrous flirtation with it (in which, for example,
recently arrived Vietnamese boat people were kept out of
the top schools on racial grounds in favour of less-well
qualified middle class Afro-American students).

Education is important for all sorts of reasons, and
educational achievements, if real, are real achievements. But the key qualification is, if real. One of the
criteria of real achievement is that people can fail, and
one sign of a system with real standards is that, hard as it
is, people do fail. Not that failure is necessarily unkind in
the medium term: early failure in one direction might
impel people to try another direction more profitable and

suitable for them, which is kinder than leaving them to flounder on in something they are not really suited for and in which they will ultimately fail.

The very idea of a system which guarantees achievement for all is a nonsense, which can only debase and downgrade real achievement. It will end up, as the British educational system is perilously close to doing, by yielding achievement for none. And this lack of real achievement is very serious, and at the most basic levels. Despite endless scares about the low level of literacy and numeracy over the past two decades, and endless governmental initiatives to improve matters, an independent study by the Curriculum, Evaluation and Management Centre from the University of Durham, confirmed by the Statistics Commission, suggest that the government's own figures greatly exaggerate the extent of any improvement (where, according to the studies, a third of 11 year olds are failing in Maths to reach the expected level and two fifths in English.) Even on the government's own figures a fifth of primary school leavers fail to reach the expected level in reading and a quarter in arithmetic, no preparation whatever for the transition to secondary school. It is blindlingly obvious to all outside the system that these failures are related to the way the basic skills of reading and arithmetic are taught (or more accurately not taught), with more concern for pupils' self esteem than for rigour. Ultimately, of course, the self-esteem of the illiterate and innumerate is irreparably damaged by an education system which has let them down and which is very largely responsible for their plight.

But the most extraordinary transformation we have seen in education over the past three or four decades is not abandonment of rigorous methods of teaching or erosion of content in the subjects which are taught. It is something which is hardly ever mentioned in surveys of the educational scene or in policy discussions. I refer to the virtual disappearance in our schools and universities of the study of the classics of ancient Greece and Rome—not that these classics were ever conceived in such narrow terms. On and off, for two and a half millennia, our culture had been animated by the potency of the myths originally explored in Homer, Hesiod and the ancient tragedies. Every age which considered itself civilised rediscovered these sources for itself, and reinvented them in its own terms. In Western Europe since the time of the European renaissance in the fourteenth and fifteenth centuries until now, you could not consider yourself an educated person unless you had familiarity with the classics. Dark ages were precisely those where classical learning did not exist, and even they were sometimes enlightened by Christianity, with classical learning kept alive in a few monasteries and libraries, and, remarkably, in parts of the Islamic world.

The nearest the general public gets to classical learning is through programmes like the BBC's series *Rome*. Inevitably, it seems, in the first episode there is full-frontal nudity, explicit sex and from Caesar's niece language racy enough to make a centurion blush. According to its writer of the series, 'one of the joys of the Roman value system for us now is that it is modern man unmasked'. So, 'everything we secretly wish for—to humiliate our enemies, to be adored by the masses, to have sex with whomsoever we want, to take what we like—all the sado-masochistic elements of human nature were in the open in the Roman world' (and no doubt in the series too).

Well, yes; all that was a part of Roman world at the beginning of the Empire. You only have to read Suetonius to see it. But that world, the same world depicted in plonking historical detail by the BBC, was also the world which produced—and admired—Virgil, Horace, Ovid, Tacitus, Livy, Lucan, Seneca, Vitruvius (and architecture to match) and Pliny. It was the world, which for all its undoubted excesses, cruelty and social disorder (see Suetonius), also produced a hitherto unknown degree of unity, order, public works and law throughout the known world for several centuries. It was the world in which Christianity eventually flourished and took root. Its eventual demise (in the West at least) was regarded by civilised people of the time as an unmitigated disaster, which would be hard to understand if Suetonius and *Rome* were the whole story.

It was for the perpetuation of classical learning in the round that the grammar schools were invented in this country, and this they did with reasonable success for four or five hundred years, and without, in the later stages of their existence, falling down on science and maths. As a nation we decided to abolish the grammar schools in the

1960s, and though some 163 of the original 2,000 remain, abolition of the institutions actually did something far more insidious than simply closing down avenues of opportunity for the academic. We also abolished the spirit of the foundation of the grammar schools, even in the independent schools formally untouched by the reforms. In 2003 675,000 pupils sat 5.7 million papers at GCSE level. Of these 5.7 million, less than 10,000 were in Latin and barely 1,000 in Greek, with another 4,447 in the non-linguistic 'Classical Civilisation' paper. The percentage in the case of Greek is so small that it actually registers as 0.0% on the official statistics. All in all, then, little chance of classical learning for the vast majority, beyond the sensationalism of the mass media.

Rousseau's own admiration for the Roman republic notwithstanding, classical learning does not easily fit in with his educational philosophy or with that inspired by Dewey's followers. For them, what is important is not learning, but 'learnacy' or learning how to learn. In *Schools in the Learning Age*[8] launched with a ringing endorsement from David Blunkett, then Secretary of State for Education, the directors of the government funded 'Campaign for Learning' tell us in Deweyesque terms that 'schools as we know them are fast becoming an anachronism'.

In today's 'turbulent society' schools should become learning centres, supporting community projects, lifelong learning and multiple modes of learning. They should adopt a competence or skills based curriculum, rather than a knowledge based one (because we cannot know in advance what knowledge will be needed in the future). Children (learners) will take responsibility for their own learning, as we saw with Sir Christopher Ball. In this new world, teachers will be 'managers, not arbiters, of learning'. They will no longer be experts in particular subject areas. Rather they will be 'experts in helping young people understand how they learn, supporting (rather than directing and correcting) their learning and, of course, geared to meeting the needs 'of the emerging e-generations'. And these needs include individuals managing a shifting set of identities, which 'might include anything from our race, gender, sexuality or religious beliefs, to our shopping or television preferences'.

Unsurprisingly, given its Deweyesque roots, there is no thought in any of this to providing a cultural inheritance for the young, or to instilling in them any sense of piety towards their and our past, or even knowledge of it. The amazing thing is that the very same people who advocate learnacy in schools rather than knowledge are then dismayed when they find they are breeding generation with no loyalty to their roots or to their country. They do not realise than the one must follow the other.

But even on their own terms, the Campaign for Learning and advocates of learnacy are misguided. One cannot know how to learn if one's mind is not already stocked by plenty of learning. We all know, most of us from our own experience, what a magnificent resource the internet is—if you know how to look and how to sift through what is there. And we also know how disastrous pinballing the internet is for those without knowledge or culture or the type of judgement which comes only from a fund of knowledge and culture. Without that we are simply unable to evaluate the worth of what they find, or even to understand what it might be they are looking for. We become easy prey to every kind of lunacy, prejudice, obsession, falsity and worse.

Far from rendering the acquisition in school of soundly based knowledge unnecessary, as proponents of learnacy maintain, the internet and its electronic off-shoots, to say nothing of the bewildering array of choices now available to young people, make the formal acquisition of knowledge in school all the more necessary in order to make sensible discriminations between the good, the less good and the downright disastrous. Nor is it true that knowledge is changing so fast that anything we learn now will be out-dated in a few years. This is obviously false in the case of literature and the humanities more generally, but no one is going to waste their time learning the science of Darwin or Cantor or Einstein or even Newton. Conversely, someone unacquainted with the rudiments of contemporary science, however well-provided with data, will be ill placed to judge if or when some new scientific insight is genuine or worthwhile.

With the virtual abolition in its schools of Greek and Latin, we have also expelled the basic languages and vocabulary of humane learning, and consequently of what have been the furnishings and images of learning of our culture for two millennia or more. There is, no doubt, ideological prejudice against Greek and Latin, but one suspects that the real reason they have vanished from our educational landscape is that learning them is hard and, in the early stages, their use uncertain. As well as implying that there are things beyond the Cave's own fantasies which one should know, the very notion of classical learning offends its ideology of reward without effort, an ideology by now well bedded down in its educational apparatus.

In fact, it is not only classical learning in the technical sense of Greek and Latin which is disparaged in today's educational world. Those who advocate a curriculum based on high culture, focusing on English literature, history, classical music, Christian doctrine and traditional knowledge and techniques and the sciences are categorised by many in the educational world as 'cultural restorationists'; the curriculum they espouse is 'the curriculum of the dead', curriculum 'as musuem'; while learning in this context is alienation, intrinsic difficulty and the negation of the self, involving abasement, passivity and deference.[9]

One wonders what people who think write this understand by the notion of renaissance; what they would make of the idea that creativity is best released by engagement with the canonical and difficult works of the past; or whether they would understand the poignancy and beauty of Dante's encounter with the shades of the pagan past in the First Circle of Hell, or of the descent of Aeneas into the underworld. If the losses were only those of Professors Ball and Brown, it would not matter much. Unfortunately these views are only too symptomatic of the sentimental fantasy running education today.

This was shown only too clearly when in 1993 over 600 university teachers on English complained that the government's attempt to make Shakespeare and a small number unspecified examples of pre-20th century literature a compulsory part of the national curriculum was 'philistine'. Even worse, it was acting 'in gross and wilful ignorance of more than two decades of intellectual debate', threatening to strip English of what is 'most precious and educational about it', and (surprise, surprise) reducing 'a vital literary heritage to a mummified relic'.

To all this one can only reply that if Shakespeare or Dickens or Keats become mummified relics in a secondary school, the fault is the teacher's, not the government's; and that it would be a pretty impoverished (philistine ?) version of English which stuck with the types of writing with which the pupils were already familiar. What the signatories of the letter did not acknowledge was that prior to the national curriculum proposals, school inspectors had found many English courses in schools 'trivial and undemanding', precisely because those teaching them preferred not to give their pupils anything 'difficult' or anything beyond their own experience. The curriculum was being suited to the child, in other words, rather than the child to the curriculum, and even after the introduction of the 'philistine' national curriculum probably to a large extent still is.

It is not just content, whether in the sciences or the humanities, which has been eroded by our educational fantasies. In making the child the centre of the educational process rather than what has to be learned, we have also skewed the relationship between pupil and teacher. To illustrate this erosion, consider the following comment from a teacher in a primary school, presented as an example of good practice in an Open University text book: 'I worry that children are always looking for the right answer. They've got a feeling that somewhere there's the right answer and only if we knew it, everything will be all right... What I want them to realise is that there's any right answer for them, and they have to decide on what it is... they have a right to decide what they think about things.' This is justified by the authors of the book in terms of problematising knowledge, of children learning how knowledge is socially constructed and of maintaining in classrooms atmospheres of critique and emotion (which are apparently good things). And, in the same book, a science teacher for 5 to 7 year olds (!) advocates giving children an opportunity to follow their own ideas, rather than focusing on facts, laws and existing understanding.[10]

Thoughts about condescension and sheep without shepherds come to mind. But there is nothing new under the sun. Long ago Plato foresaw a stage in civilisation in which the teacher would no longer be recognised as an authority and respected as such: 'the schoolmaster timidly flatters his pupils and pupils make light of their masters; the old, anxious not to be thought disagreeable tyrants imitate the young and condescend to enter into their jokes and amusements'. Our teachers, even of very young children, are apparently quite happy to fit into the Platonic picture, in which they abrogate any claim to knowledge or authority.

This, of course, is not the worst of it. If teachers are not authorities about what they are supposed to be teaching, but merely facilitators, 'problematising knowledge', forvever debating the worth of the curriculum, disparaging the great works of the past, denying the existence of right answers (even in science) and simply helping children to make their own decisions as to what is right, how can they claim any moral authority over their pupils? Hardly surprising, then, that we are now in a situation in which many schools resemble battlegrounds rather than places of learning, and even in those which are not battlegrounds, the balance of power has shifted catastrophically from teacher to pupil. Teachers have connived in all this, doubtless for the best and most sentimental of reasons, wanting not to challenge or upset their pupils, but the results are catastrophic.

It is not just that pupils, left to their own enquiries, discover very little, and remain ignorant. Worse, perhaps, facilitating, as opposed to teaching, is not a role which demands great respect from pupils; an erosion of the respect due to teachers is almost inevitable if pupils are encouraged to believe that their ideas are as good as anyone else's and that knowledge is a social construct negotiated by partners. But one thing they do know is that as a result of misguided child-centred legal reforms and educational policies, legally it is almost impossible to discipline them if they are not willing to be disciplined. Pupils have it in their power to ruin the career of a teacher they do not like by a careless or malicious complaint. In many schools violence against teachers is commonplace, and yet, to foster the illusion of 'inclusion', the government and the law make it albeit impossible to expel pupils. In these circumstances, the wonder is not that standards have declined, but that anything is actually learned at all. Nor is it any surprise that two fifths A and B grades at A level come from the 9% of pupils educated in independent and grammar schools, places in the educational world where there is still some semblance of respect for knowledge.

8

SPEECH STALINISM

The experience machine is an attempt to have the benefit of what we all need and want without actually going to the trouble of getting it, overlooking the fact that the trouble of getting it is a crucial part of what constitutes the benefit. So are drugs. Egalitarianism is the pretence that all can have what, by definition and nature, only a few can achieve. Celebrities are the floss of egalitarianism, people who have achieved fame and riches without accomplishment of any particularly worthwhile kind. And the notion of entertainment, so pervasive in our lives, aims to obliterate all distinctions of quality.

Living in the Cave makes much of this hard to perceive, a difficulty compounded by the language of the Cave. For the language of the Cave attempts to enlist the vocabulary of real achievement to clothe emptiness and mediocrity.

In some ways this was what happened in the Eastern bloc under communism. Words were used in an entirely post-modernist spirit. That is to say, they bore no relation to anything outside themselves. They referred to nothing other than other words, and certainly not to things or achievements in the real world. Five year plans in industry were accomplished and targets in agriculture were met, even though there were shortages everywhere and mass starvation. And indeed failures of language were not unrelated to the failures in performance they were constructed to disguise.

Nor was this systematic mendacity without effect on people's souls. Vaclav Havel has written with great insight on the effect such thoroughgoing pretence has on those who are party to it. Even while applauding the 'successes' of the regime, which they had to do regularly and ritually, ordinary people in communist Czechoslovakia knew the truth. That, though, would not necessarily stop them denouncing those who spoke the truth in their hearing, for people's jobs and their children's education and future often depended on active complicity in the lie. Those who wrote the documents and articles which endorsed the lie did not believe what they wrote either. Nor even did the rulers. Yet all, except the so-called dissidents, connived actively and passively in the lying and corruption, just to have a peaceful life. Iron entered their souls and civil society was, and in many cases still is, undermined.

Comparisons between our situation and state socialism may seem far fetched, and in some ways perhaps they are. On the whole people in this country are not sent to the mad-house or prison for dissent. But in one crucial sense comparisons between us and them are not misplaced. In public life, and in commerce and industry, and in our jobs, we are all complicit in systematic lying and Orwellian doublespeak, so much so that we probably hardly even notice it.

What we do notice are the very public instances when politicians at the top of the political ladder are caught out in some more egregious example of spin, economy with the actualité, difficulty wielding the 'simple sword of truth and the trusty shield of fair play', and even worse, the lie direct. Many of us are quick to condemn these abuses, even believing that, in distinction to what goes on in our own lives, they should be a focus of shame.

There is undoubtedly a degree of sanctimoniousness about this. Pointing this out is not to say that politicians and the like should not be more honourable than in fact they are, or to condone the extent of the duplicity which no doubt infects public life. No doubt politicians should be more honourable. But dishonour is far more pervasive than the well trumpeted failures of politicians. Many of those making judgements about politicians will themselves have been quite prepared in their own jobs to go along with all kinds of claims and promises they could not possibly believe.

Take, for example, the use of the word 'excellent'. There can hardly be an institution, in either public or private sectors, which does not declare that it and all its employees and administrators are excellent, or, if not actually quite excellent yet, are 'striving for excellence'. This is, of course, in the literal sense pointless. Without specifying what activity is in question, one cannot simply be excellent or strive for excellence. Excellent in which respect? Excellence in which sphere?

Once the sphere is specified, we know what it is the institution is doing. And are we to suppose that it is aiming to do whatever it is doing in an unsatisfactory way, or that doing it badly would be its aim? And if, as by definition, most institutions are at best mediocre and are filled with second-rate people (and better that than poor and third-rate), are we to think that prating about excellence is actually going to alter anything? As Spinoza observed, excellence is as difficult as it is rare.

On the principle that good wine needs no bush, one might suppose that it will be precisely those institutions which are genuinely excellent (by definition, necessarily only a few, the ones which excel) which will talk the least about excellence. In that case, we could safely conclude that whenever an institution proclaimed its own excellence, it was actually no better than average or mediocre.

Unfortunately, such is the corruption of our manners and language in 2005 that one would not be surprised if these days even universities like Oxford and Cambridge, schools like St Paul's and institutions like the Royal Opera House, which really are excellent, would be tempted to produce glossy documents proclaiming their excellence (or even worse, their commitment to excellence, as if excellence was something one could be committed to, rather than be accorded in virtue of one's innate ability and actual achievements, as recognised by others, things rather outside one's control).

But, were they to succumb to the temptation, who would they be telling these things to? Who, who has any interest in the matter or the slightest knowledge of it would need to be told? If they are true, people will know anyway, and if they are not, being told they are will not help. Being told in a dirty and disease-ridden hospital or on a over-crowded five hour late train or plane that the Chief Executive and all his staff are all 'committed to excellence' actually only compounds the insult, making a mockery of the doubtless valiant efforts made in damage limitation by some at least of those on the ground. In just the same way, it seems doubly insulting to be told that a university is committed to excellence in teaching when you are actually taught not individually or in small groups by the big names (if any), but in huge classes and by under-qualified part-timers. Is the idea that people in the Cave are more stupid than peasants in Soviet Russia in the 1930s and cannot see what is before their eyes?

Maybe they can't, because the talk goes on, wherever one looks. An example taken at random from documents currently on my desk (but serving to exemplify a particular type of pronouncement from organisations of all types, public and private): 'The teaching profession has never been in better shape. Teaching standards—already high—have been improving year on year, and the effect can be seen in schools, in pupils' performance.' These words appeared above the signature of the then Secretary of State for Education. He did not mention there that under his predecessor primary schools had failed to meet the government's relatively modest targets in English and maths for 11 year olds. But in 2003, he did himself postpone national targets for 11 year olds for a couple of years (until after a forthcoming general election, in other words) and announce a re-vamping of the tests for 7 year olds. In like mode, after the unbelievable A level results of 2005, Lord Adonis, the education minister proclaimed that 'our young people as a whole are being much better taught, their aspirations are much higher and their performance is improving accordingly.'

Does anyone in teaching, actually in a staff room, believe that 'the teaching profession has never been in better shape'? In 2004, teacher turnover in primary schools was 14.7% of which 10% was wastage, and in secondary schools the figure were 12.5% and 7.2% respectively, with early retirements rising by 40% since 2002 and accounting for a third of head teacher resignations. No doubt the teachers not committed to excellence (or to testing, of whom there are still a great many) might be cheered up by the suspension of targets; but judging by the complaints teachers universally and endlessly—and not always unjustifiably—make about funding, about colleagues (often the best) leaving in droves, about bureaucracy, about the doubts we have already considered concerning the validity of the government's measures of improvement and inflating exam grades, about the indiscipline of pupils, about the very real stress and worse brought about by the often groundless and malicious complaints of pupils, about problems with unsupportive and objectionable parents, and much else besides, it is hard to believe that anyone could seriously claim that the profession as a whole is in better shape. Does anyone who knows about education, without a vested interest in it, who compares the demands now in exams with those of 30 or 40 years ago, actually agree with Lord Adonis? So, how can these things be said without apparently a hint of embarrassment? How can there be such a degree of cognitive dissonance, so to speak, between what is said by those in charge and what 'everyone' knows?

Along with excellence goes quality, and along with quality goes quality assurance. It is because of inspection evidence produced largely by mechanisms of 'quality assurance' that officials, politicians and chief executives, very likely sincerely, are able to claim that all is well, and that services, public and private, are better than ever and getting better all the time.

The first thing to realise about quality assurance is that it has absolutely nothing to do with quality, but it has everything to do with management. And on the basis that those who do, can, and those who cannot, manage, it would be unwise to expect anything of practical use coming out of quality assurance—except, of course, things of practical use to the managers, of which the first is more importance and status for them, the second a device for controlling subordinates and the third a tool with which to reassure a gullible public.

As an example of quality assurance in practice, I take my own experience of being inspected by the Government's Quality Assurance Agency (for higher education). This is not, I should emphasize, sour grapes. My department actually scored the highest possible mark, 24 out of 24, and was the first department to be so ranked both in my (then) university and in my subject. Nor is my quarrel with the inspectors themselves, who were impeccably fair and professional. My quarrel is with the process itself, a process which is almost entirely focused on process.

One might have thought that inspecting a small academic department in a university would be a fairly simple business. There are, perhaps, three things which are important to know, and which an inspection ought to reveal. First, is what the department is teaching worth teaching? Second, are its students well taught? And third, in a climate where there are widespread worries about slipping standards, how do its standards today compare with standards earlier? All this could be easily ascertained by some respected academics sitting in on a few classes and taking a quick look at sets of finals papers over a few years. But nothing in quality assurance is so elegant or straightforward.

Under the quality assurance regime, two out of our

three questions are not dealt with at all, and the third only marginally. The body being inspected is judged not by any external standard, or indeed by a close scrutiny of the results of its work, but by means a 'self-assessment' document, which it writes itself. So, the question as to whether what it teaches is worth teaching does not come up. So long as the department does what it says it is doing (e.g. investigating racial and sexual stereotyping in Australian soap operas), it is going to be all right (very convenient, of course, for those teaching non-subjects, but not necessarily what the general public would expect to be told about an activity not worth doing at all). Nor, in an inspection based on self-assessment is the question of standards over time going to arise, unless a department is foolish enough to claim in its self-assessment that its standards now are better than they were earlier. Teaching is observed in the inspection, but the results of such observation play a very small role in the process as a whole, and I am not clear that the standards students achieved in their final examinations played any role at all.

What plays the major role in quality assurance is whether you are able to provide evidence that you are doing what you say in the self-assessment document, and as evidence means documentation, a forty page self-assessment document has to be backed up by a room full of documents (literally), 'proving' that all your claims are underwritten by formal procedures, university committees, minuted meetings, resolutions, targets set and met (or, if not met, by further procedures to examine why they had not been met), and also that everything you do in the way of altering the course even in the minutest detail is approved by layers of university bureaucracy, and their approval fed back to the department and noted in its committees. Terribly important was 'closing the quality loop': that is to say, if, for example, an external examiner made a comment after some exams, this comment had to go upwards through the university machinery, and then downwards again to the department, where it would be acted on, the acting on noted, and so on and so on, into, one presumes, another quality loop.

You will also have to show that you have 'policies' 'in place' and targets set to deal with disabilities, equal opportunities (how you are in effect moving towards quotas in various directions), health and safety, staff development, dealing with complaints, procedures for appointment of new staff, and all the other items of social engineering beloved of the twenty-first century bureaucrat. This all goes to make up what has become known as the government's agenda, but none of this agenda begins to touch on the essence on what one should be doing (actually, neither more nor less than teaching one's subject with knowledge and enthusiasm). Nothing in quality assurance has any bearing whatever on the actual quality of what you do, except in the negative sense of the entangling us all in ever more quality loops, target setting, tiresome meetings, self-important committees and jargon-ridden paperwork. All these trails and many others the inspectors were expected to follow in their excavations in the 'base room' (the room full of documents).

The inspectors did occasionally emerge from the dust and gloom of their base room, observe the odd lecture and talk to us or to our students. But for the most part they were incarcerated in their room (to which only they had a key), poring over files, ticking boxes, shuffling documents, and no doubt trying to close quality loops. Had they been seated on high stools, they would have been the modern day equivalents of Dickensian clerks.

It is, I suppose, possible that some utterly hopeless department might have had some of its more blatant inadequacies exposed by this sort of process, but at what a cost in time, money and effort all round; but such a department and its host university would have had to be truly awful. We all knew a year before the inspection that the inspectors were coming, and, with the help of the university's own internal bureaucracy, the vast majority of departments would be able to cover their tracks in most areas and produce (in both senses) 'evidence' of their procedures. But let us suppose that the procedures were already as impeccable as they could be, and had not been fudged up in the last few months before the inspection. Would that show that decisions which had been taken had been wise, that courses offered were good ones, that standards had not slipped over the years with greater numbers of less well qualified students, or that students actually got a good deal?

Of course it would not; all it would show is that procedures had been followed and bureaucratic targets met, and in that sense and in that sense only 'quality' is assured by the inspection. And one can certainly think of cases where the very best academics, such as Wittgenstein or F.R. Leavis or Freddie Ayer would have fallen foul of the quality police precisely because of their single minded commitment to their subject and to the education of their pupils, even at the expense of procedures. For at least some of their courses they would not, as is now required, have written out their syllabus in advance, or even less, would they have been prepared to specify the learning outcomes and transferable skills students would acquire from the course, if only because they would have followed the intellectual trail on which they and their students were embarking, to whatever 'outcome' it might lead, and also because of a well justified suspicion of the very concept of a transferable skill.

Yet—and this is the point about Stalinist complicity—while very many academics would agree with most of what I have just written, even if in less forthright terms, I know of only one in the whole country who refused to take part in the exercise, and it was only late in the day (and after some poor results) that an institution publicly proclaimed itself dissatisfied with the procedure. Nearly everyone, in other words, including, I have to admit, myself, went along with the exercise, and this in an arena supposedly committed to free enquiry and intellectual integrity.

I do not for a moment suppose that quality assurance in universities is much different from quality assurance anywhere else. So next time we hear teachers in schools talking about being over-burdened with paper work (so as to gird their loins, or those of their superiors, for their next OFSTED inspection), or, after some crisis, a public official talking about instituting better 'procedures' to ensure that such a thing never happens again, or, in order to convince the public that the public services are really getting better, a government minister talks of instituting 'targets', we should remember that the context is one of 'quality assurance'. And we should remember, too, that the things which really count, in education or medicine or most other fields, things like integrity, honesty, wisdom, inspiration, real knowledge and practical intelligence, are not measurable or specifiable as 'targets': so targets are invented and massaged, as in the manipulation of health service waiting times, and in ways which have little to do with real quality.

And we should also remember that targets are always supposed to be improvements on what is actually the case, which may be easy enough for poor institutions to fulfil, but which produce some odd anomalies in institutions already genuinely good. (Thus a school where 100% of pupils get 5 A to C grades at GCSE one year and only 99.5% do so the next year will be shown in government statistics as having added 'less value' than one that has 6% one year and 9% the next; the first school will also be shown as having failed to meet its target in contrast to the other which is trumpeted by government ministers as one of the most improved schools in the country; but if you are a parent, which school would you prefer to send your child to?)

In sum the last thing which quality assurance assures is quality (which explains why inspectors and politicians are able to claim that teaching and the teaching profession have never been in better shape, when these things are so obviously not true). But what quality assurance does do is to institute huge bureaucracies inside and outside the institutions whose quality is being assured, with all the waste, replication and sheer redundant paperwork these things spawn, to say nothing of obsession with irrelevant and counter-productive targets. (Teachers and health service workers are not wrong when they whinge about management, because it is the ideology and practice of quality assurance which currently counts as 'managing'.)

Even worse, quality assurance also protects stupidity and mediocrity by enabling the stupid and the mediocre to defend themselves against any criticism or liability by claiming, in all probability correctly, that 'procedures' have been followed and 'policies' implemented, never mind that the procedures and policies are to a large extent pointless or worse. And worse even than that, but as a result of its cumulative effect, quality assurance drives out real talent and real judgement by insisting that long experience and practical wisdom are not only not enough, but have to have the life squeezed out of them by being fitted on to a Procrustean bed of 'aims', 'objectives', 'skills' and 'intended outcomes'.

As well as excellence, which is not excellence and quality, which is not quality, we have access which is not access. The three things are, in fact, connected. Not only are they all part of the government's 'agenda', but part of what is meant by both excellence and by quality is a commitment to 'access'. Indeed, one of the things you will undoubtedly have to show in assuring quality is that you have 'in place' policies which guarantee access. Access, indeed, has become one of the greatest fantasies of the age, one which merits a chapter on its own.

9

ACCESS

Access in its original sense refers to physical layout. There is, it would be said, no access by road to the summit of Snowdon, though (against all principles of ecology and conservation) there is access by rail. There is no wheelchair access down the cliffs to Treen Beach, which is said to be a BAD THING (because it means that the disabled can't get there). And it is such a bad thing, that at great financial and aesthetic cost thousands of historic buildings and steps, to say nothing of millions of pavements, have been despoiled so as to introduce ramps, which are in practice barely used. One is not, of course, supposed to question any of this—access for all to all places is taken to be as unquestioned a good as, say, hostility to racism and sexism; though, before he died, Quentin Crewe, the wheel-chair bound writer, did question whether every castle in the country really had to be opened up in this way so that he might tour its battlements. Are there not enough castles and buildings opened up already, and, we might add, what about all the

151

sites and sights accessible only to the young, the slim and the fit (which surely amounts to discrimination against the fat, the aged and the unfit)? And, as in the case of the Snowdon railway, might there not be other considerations militating against access for all (even were such a thing ever really possible)?

However, physical access is not now the big point, though it is quite big enough. The big point in our fantasy world is that nothing intellectual or cultural must be inaccessible to anyone, because that would be elitism, militating against inclusivity (another of the age's sacred cows). So all institutions of learning, as well as museums, art galleries, concert halls and opera houses, if they want public or charitable funding, have to have access policies, education schemes, outreach programmes and much else besides. Above all they must be fun, they must attract the young, minorities and those who have never shown any interest in such things before. They must at all costs avoid looking expensive or exclusive (though none can be as expensive or exclusive as a top show, pop concert or football match). And the thought that some things are so precious or difficult or rare that the mass public should be dissuaded from contaminating them with its noisy, ignorant, hamburger-eating and litter-strewing presence is, in the arts world of 2005, as close to heresy as one could get. Certainly no one overheard expressing such a view, even half in jest and eminently sensible as the view is, will get anywhere a job in the arts or funding for any project he or she might have, however worthwhile it might be.

There are, indeed, two ways of approaching works of high culture and those of the past. One can approach them by the way of culture, which is to admit our ignorance and to learn their language, their concepts and their ways. Or one can approach them by the way of entertainment, the Disney way, the theme park way, the Hollywood way, the access way. This is to treat them as a way of illustrating what we already know, embellishing the notions we already have, and of providing themes and locations for our own stories and thoughts. This way involves no effort, and this is the way of the typical access or outreach project. You make a difficult work accessible, reducing its difficulty or stature so that it neither intimidates nor challenges the mentality of the day. In doing this, one in effect simply plunders the past or high culture for effects and local colour.

It can be rewarding in its own way. Even a Disneyland castle may be more impressive than the average modern building; even a Hollywood epic might intimate a form of life different from our own, and in some ways superior to our own; even producing Shakespeare as if it were soap opera might be a little better than EastEnders.

But if that is where it ends, one learns as little from it as one learns from tourism (and nothing narrows the mind as much as tourism in its implication that peoples and cultures differ only superficially and can be grasped in their essence by travel alone). Generally speaking, in Hollywood epics one hardly gets beyond the clichés about the past on which the theme park is predicated (and that is assuming that there is no deliberate falsification of the past, as is all too common in the way current Hollywood productions attempt to avoid offending modern sensibilities). Access projects, too, are so concerned with demonstrating the 'relevance' of some work from the past or high culture that one misses out on its essence, which is precisely to be different from and deeper that the clichés and prejudices of the present

The way of culture is quite different. Imagine a savage hearing for the first time, Caliban like, civilised music, 'sounds and sweet airs, that give delight and hurt not'. This Caliban might, of course, be a youth of today, in the early morning stumbling out of the inferno of a club or disco, where, over several hours, his senses had been bombarded and his sensibility systematically ravaged, and overhearing some ethereal spirits singing a madrigal in the early morning. Like Caliban, he might be entranced, and begin see a way other than that of rap and hip-hop… 'in dreaming / the clouds methought would open and show riches / ready to drop upon me, that when I wak'd / I cried to dream again'.

But to grasp this dream, to hold these hints, one has to enter the palace of culture on its own terms, in a spirit of reverence and humility—the very opposite of that spirit of grasping and patronised ignorance implied by talk of access, and the very opposite to the way our own cultural elite like to present themselves and the heritage they are supposed to be conveying. In August 2005,

Glyndebourne announced that it was proposing to stage a 'hiphop' version of Mozart's *Cosi Fan Tutte*. Apparently the scene will be shifted from Naples in the 18th century to a London housing estate with the main characters roadies embarking on a rap tour. As well as reworking Mozart's music with sampled drum beats and pulsating bass lines, the audience will see graffiti 'artists' and break dancers at work. Glyndebourne's 'head of education' feebly comments that Mozart was young himself, and the theme of the constancy of lovers is itself constant. Well... One of the 'creative consultants' of the project is quoted as saying that 'traditional British people have to start re-examining themselves and their culture in terms of addressing the new age.' There we have the authentic voice of today's art bureaucrat, at once wheedling, dogmatic and vaguely threatening. All in all it would be hard to parody the ways of our artistic administrators and not really very funny. What is sure is that Mozart's music is what is of the essence, and that should be allowed to speak as it is—whether or not it appeals to those whose taste is rap. It is just that which the so-called 'hiphopera' will deny them.

In 1856 Hector Berlioz was in the midst of composing *The Trojans*. It was a theme which had obsessed him since he first started reading *The Aeneid* in Latin with his father at the age of ten. He wrote to his sister that 'working at my opera intoxicates me, as the composition of *Romeo and Juliet* did ten years ago. I swim with strong strokes in the lake of antique poetry. What gratitude we

155

owe to these great spirits, those mighty hearts, who gave us such noble emotions as they speak to us across the centuries. It seems to me that I've known Virgil and Shakespeare, that I can see them.'

Gratitude, mighty hearts, noble emotions, voices across centuries, swimming in the lake of antique poetry, seeing Virgil and Shakespeare… and so entering a realm so unlike our own that we ourselves are elevated and transformed. But the condition of any such transformation is that we first listen to them, rather than bending them to our own will and intelligence, and leading them around like captives on a rope. But perhaps because in our small-minded timidity we are scared of notions such as nobility and gratitude, and frightened by the very idea of antique poetry, perhaps because cannot bear the thought of anything higher than life in the Cave, that is just what, all too often, we do. Thus the National Gallery in London, having already destroyed the subtlety and even the colour of Titian's *Bacchus and Ariadne* by cleaning it in the spirit of an age brasher than Titian's own, is now attempting to drum up popular interest in the painting by dubbing it an illustration of 'the greatest chat-up line ever', as if anyone would be drawn really to look at the painting, and to fall under its magnetism, by such obviously patronising piffle.

Nor can our cultural panjandrums resist degrading *The Trojans* itself; Aeneas, according to Virgil, like 'the lord Apollo in the spring' with his hair bound 'in fronded laurel, braided in gold', walking 'with sunlit grace upon him', this son of Venus, portrayed as a shaven headed punk; Dido, Sidonian Dido, Queen of Carthage, clothed in gold and scarlet, according to Virgil,—in a business suit, their cave being simply a trap door in the stage, the Romans boorish mercenaries, and no great palace or hall filled with mementoes of Troy (this last a crucial part of the story for both Virgil and Berlioz), but a set of such deliberate ugliness as to expunge from our minds any thought of the Carthage of antiquity or of Turner's great painting or of the *pietas* of Aeneas and his Trojan troops. (That, presumably, was its point.) Were it not for the music itself, which received an adequate performance, it might be that the English National Opera Company, in its recent performance of *The Trojans* had actually wanted to keep its audience in ignorance of the work's meaning and potential, as if such untimely thoughts were too subversive and politically incorrect to be permitted on a public stage.

The theatrical directors and gallery curators responsible for aberrations such as these will say that one has to present every work of the past so as to connect with our own time. They are wrong. In what they say and do they show that they are themselves incapable of learning from the works of the past, whose greatness and meaning is precisely that though they are not of our time they are, in themselves, capable of speaking to our time and all times. They are capable of elevating us. It is just this possibility we seem intent on closing off. We reduce high art and its ambition to entertainment and to political correctitude in which equality and inclusivity deny any distinctions of quality or ambition. We transform it into the very image of contemporary life which we need to be raised from. In so doing we diminish both ourselves and our culture. We wrap ourselves more impermeably in the cocoons of our fantasies.

And so, in the name of 'access' a thousand museums, galleries and concert halls dumb themselves down to look like nursery schools. Top universities scour the worst schools in the country to persuade ill-qualified youngsters to give them a try. It is all a pretence. No one will ever enter the worlds of high culture or learning who is not prepared and who does not work at the preparation. Milton, let us say, will not reveal his secrets to people who do not steep themselves in the Bible and the classics, any more than will Titian, tosh about chat-up lines notwithstanding. You cannot listen to Beethoven or Mozart as if they were pop or rap, and hope to get anything out of the music. They demand, and repay, attention, concentration and even study, though if you give them the time, they will blow your mind in a way the detritus of the mass media never can. And it is not implausible to believe that Einstein, T.S. Eliot and Kant will forever be beyond the grasp of the great majority of people.

Nor indeed should we expect everyone appreciate the same things. But it is an unspoken premises of 'access' that there must be no book closed to anyone (or, in the name of equality, steps will be taken to close it to everyone).

But, once brought to light, there seems no valid reason for this assumption. Tastes, interests and abilities differ. I might think that someone without artistic appreciation is impoverished to that extent, but it is not clear that this means that he or she has to be cajoled, bribed or titillated into going into an art gallery or opera house, any more than equity demands that I be made to go to a rap concert or a football match, and particularly not where the means to do so fundamentally mis-represents the experience. It is also inherently patronising and conde-scending to the recipients of access programmes, in that it assumes that people on south London housing estates are inherently less capable of appreciating Mozart of Beethoven than people like me, who came from a boring suburb on the edge of Epping Forest. Beethoven, whole, entire and unadulterated, in the honest, intense and urgent performances characteristic of the 1950s, blew my world apart and gave me perspectives and possibilities I had not even dreamed of, so why should he not be able to do it for someone from Lewisham or Brixton?

I cannot resist closing this chapter with a passage from Berlioz's memoirs. After giving a lurid description of the vulgarity, violence and sheer trashiness of the Roman carnival of 1831, of its 'bloated days, greasy with mire and sweat and grinning painted faces, gross with brutalities, ... the boredom and degradation of humanity', he says this:

'Good people! There is something very touching in your simple sport, a kind of poetry and natural dignity in your pleasures. How right they are, the great critics, when they say, Art is for all. If Raphael painted his divine madonnas, it was because he understood the exalted passion of the masses for the pure, the beautiful, the ideal. If Michelangelo wrested his immortal Moses from the bowels of the marble and raised up with his mighty hands a glorious temple, it was of course to satisfy their souls' yearning for profound emotions. It was to feed the sacred flame which burns in the hearts of the people that Tasso and Dante sang. Let all works not admired by the mob be anathema! For if it scorns them it is because they are worthless. If it holds them in contempt, it is because they are contemptible. And if it rejects them with catcalls, let the author too be rejected! He has shown a want of proper respect for the public, he has outraged its intelligence and wounded its deepest sensibilities. Away with him to the mines!'

Plus ça change. I may not be sent to the mines, but at the risk of permanent social exclusion, let me say this. The truly excellent is not accessible to all. Real quality can only be assured only by people who are exceptional at what they do; it is not producible on demand by means of managerial techniques. And only the chosen few (Stendhal's 'happy few') will ever enter the inner sanctuaries of the real palaces of the arts and of learning. These are the truths which our cult of access would conspire to hide from the general gaze, as such ideas, for all their truth, are inherently offensive to the inhabitants of the Cave.

One still wonders, though, why this should be so

offensive. After all no one suggests that everyone be made, against their will and inclination, to read the tabloids or *Hello* magazine, to watch *Big Brother* or to indulge in some other fantasy of the Cave. The offence higher art and learning present to the inhabitants of the Cave is presumably the mere existence of people who actually dislike its fantasies, and the mere suggestion that there might be more elevated tastes. It is for this reason that access programmes are all too often predicated on the assumption that what they are introducing is not really more elevated at all. And that is not just a huge mistake tactically, in that someone who is expecting to find the same sort of thing in a Titian painting as in a soap opera or in a Mozart opera as in rap music is going to be quickly disappointed; it is fundamentally dishonest, like so much in our language and culture.

We should not forget that outreach and access are currently multi-million pound industries, job-creation schemes in themselves. But their net result will be in the name of relevance and accessibility to close off the works the works of the past and of high culture from those who live in the present, and those whose horizons are (unfortunately) bounded by south London housing estates and the attendant grafitti and rap. A paradox on the surface, perhaps, access denying access; but not really a paradox when one reflects that the value of high culture and of the masterpieces of the past is that they transcend their own time, and ours.

10

SHAME

Life in the Cave, or on the experience machine, is a life of receptivity. We have experiences, and we may even choose which experiences we have, in the same way that we might flick between channels on a television set. But there is no full-bloodied engagement with a recalcitrant reality outside of us, a reality conceived as making demands on us, rather than a reality pliable and malleable in our hands. In this sense, life in the Cave will be a life without piety, as we have seen, and also a life without guilt or shame.

For many people, a guilt-free, shame-free life would be a most attractive prospect. Guilt and shame are unpleasant in themselves. In addition they are often typified as being irrational. We are guilty about sexual peccadilloes, perhaps, or about what we now think of as sexual peccadilloes, or about refusing unreasonable demands on the part of parents or other relations. We feel shame at something we cannot help, about losing a job through no fault of our own, or about some aspect of our appearance we can do nothing about. People grieving over the death of someone close sometimes have awful guilt for something done or for something not done, thus compounding their sorrow and poisoning their memories.

It is true that some people are psychologically and even physically undermined either by guilt or by shame or by both. Shame about the image of one's body can lead to terrible and even potentially fatal eating disorders. Guilt can cripple people emotionally, rendering them incapable of independent thought or action. Concentration on the pathology of guilt and shame can easily lead us into the belief that they are not just unpleasant—which they are—but that they are wholly and fundamentally negative, throwbacks to a form of life when people were terrorized by fears of ritual pollution or religious damnation.

A prevalent school of thought, doubtless influenced by Darwin, would have it that we human beings are simply animals. The notion that we have freedoms and potentialities beyond the animal is an illusion, because at the end of the day all our works and pomps and also what we are pleased high-mindedly to regard as our moral codes are to do with individual survival and repro-duction. Each of us is simply programmed to act so as to maximise our chances of survival and reproduction. Of course, some of us are better at this sort of thing than others, and so survive and reproduce more than others, and then pass on our successful characteristics to our descendents, and there are all sorts of devious ways of promoting our natural destiny, some of which we mistakenly think of as moral or honourable in themselves; but in the end the instrumentality of survival and reproduction is all there is to human life.

Add to this naturalism the psychotherapeutic nostrum that civilisation itself exacts a great psychological cost from us, individually and collectively, and we will begin to see guilt and shame in a thoroughly discreditable light. For, as the emotions whose role is to police our instincts, they become instruments of repression, denying us the natural happinesses and pleasures which arise from instinctual satisfaction; futhermore guilt and shame are themselves predicated on a view of human nature which is fundamentally erroneous (the view that there is more to human life than the satisfaction of instinct).

Life in the Cave is all about experience and happiness, cost free. So it is hardly surprising to find the guardians of the Cave decrying shame and guilt, and telling us that we should avoid being troubled by them. We are told that our first duty is to ourselves, even that the word 'should' itself is fundamentally tyrannical. What we have to do is to loosen up, chill out and be natural. We must do nothing to damage our own self-esteem or that of others. And, if individually people without shame have a greater chance of happiness than those who set themselves impossible ideals, politically a society of people unrepressed and relaxed in themselves is likely to be as close to a peaceful state of nature as we can get. Apart from anything else people unrepressed and relaxed will not bother to fight or oppress others out of a misplaced sense of duty or out intolerance of otherness, because they will have a very attenuated sense of duty and, hanging loose themselves, no hostility to otherness as such.

No doubt, on this view, law-breakers and criminals in today's repressive circumstances are more sinned against than sinning, victims of society's repressive laws and intolerance of difference. So, for example, whereas in some of the more allegedly backward states of the USA, persistent young offenders are sent to boot camps, in this country they are given non-directive therapy in circumstances of some comfort, including having their own rooms and license to be as rude as they like. The fact that our young offenders eventually emerge almost universally to re-offend unlike graduates of the boot camps, some of whom feel that the shaming experience actually built up their moral fibre and helped to put them on the road to lawfulness tends to be ignored. For us, the key point is to bolster the damaged 'self-esteem' of the young criminal, to save him from the humiliation attendant on his failing to meet 'impossible' ideals (such as not driving stolen cars at the age of 13 on the wrong side of the road while drunk—as was reported in a recent case, and where at least one MP leaped in to criticise the fact the offender had, surprisingly enough, actually been given a custodial sentence).

According to the psychotherapist Adam Phillips, impossible ideals, such as complete honesty, absolute knowledge, perfect happiness and eternal love, humiliate us.[11] These ideals are impossible, because we are not embodied angels, near the top of the great chain of being. Lives dominated by impossible ideals will be experienced as continuous failure. From the perspective of nature, the perspective of Darwin and Freud, we are creatures of nature, animals endeavouring to survive and reproduce and to be happy, though endowed with language and consciousness and an apparently sophisticated intelligence. At root, it would seem to follow from this perspective, we are no different from insects or rodents.

It is, indeed, our consciousness and intelligence which has tended to disguise this fundamental fact about ourselves and tricked us into setting ourselves impossible ideals. These ideals might have had a positive role at an earlier stage of human development when life was harder all round, but now they serve only to produce fanaticism and conflict between people, and unhappy lives filled with guilt and shame for having failed our ideals. According to Phillips, drawing on his reading of Darwin and Freud, the best possible moral progress would be for a society to diminish humiliation.

As Nietzsche might have said, and Phillips did say, there is a will to pessimism involved in setting ourselves tasks we can never accomplish. On this view we are diminished by the inevitable sense of failure which comes from setting ourselves these tasks (though little is said in these discussions about what more we achieve by having—and missing—high ideals in all sorts of fields, than we would have achieved by not having the ideals at all).

J.S. Mill famously raised the question as to whether it would be better to be Socrates dissatisfied or a fool satisfied. Mill clearly thought it would be better to be Socrates, even though his (high) ideals made satisfaction all but impossible. But for us, folly will reign. As we saw in considering our educational fantasies, a sense of failure is what must at all costs be avoided. Much counselling and psychotherapy is dedicated to alleviating our sense of failure, and to weaning us off the guilt and shame which characteristically attends failure. And we see in the Cave are any number of television programmes in which people, great and small, display their weaknesses, shamelessly, and are applauded by largely brain-dead audiences for doing so.

Shame and kindred feelings like guilt and remorse are indeed unpleasant, and, like all other emotions, can be irrational and obsessive. But it does not follow from the abuse of shame that shamelessness is a desirable state, individually or collectively, or that the diminution of humiliation is everywhere a good or indeed an ideal to be pursued above all others. The annual summer pilgrimages of British youth to places like Ibiza and Faliraki are examples of public shamelessness on a large scale, but so also were the anti-Jewish riots in Germany on Kristallnacht and the massacres of Hutus by Tutsis in Rwanda. For shamelessness occurs whenever people throw off the constraints of civilised life and, as in these examples, give vent to their instincts.

For it is shame which keeps our baser instincts in check. It is shame which makes us ashamed when we give way to them. In one sense, shame is part of what distinguishes us from animals, who do not feel shame. In disparaging shame and attempting to eradicate it from our lives, those who wish to see us as animals are quite right, from their point of view. But that does not mean that they are really right. They need to ask themselves whether someone who had participated in some drunken debauch in Faliraki and who did not afterwards feel some shame over and above their hangover would actually be a better person than someone who, after the same experience, did feel some shame; and whether it would not have been best of all if someone tempted to expose herself in the Best Bottom 2005 competition had actually walked away for fear of the shame participation in the event would later on provoke, rather than having her self-esteem bolstered by the acclaim she got for having taken part. The fact that many of those who go to such places apparently have no shame about what goes on in them is, of course, part of what is wrong.

According to Christian doctrine, in the words of St Paul, the human body is the temple of the Holy Spirit. Doubtless an impossible ideal, according to the likes of Adam Phillips. But before we reject it out of hand, we should consider the meaning of the image. A temple is, of course, a building and shares the properties of all buildings, foundations, walls, floors, etc. But a temple has a special function, higher than, say, a shed, and will be designed and decorated according to the dignity of its purpose. So the human body shares many of the properties of the bodies of animals, and can execute many of the same basic activities and purposes. But, as a temple is to a shed, so is the human body to the body of an ape. For the human body is the outward form of a person, capable of behaving with grace, dignity, intelligence, nobility and passion sublimated in the service of art.

We also, whether Christians or not, believe (still believe) that human persons should be treated with respect, with more respect indeed than animals. Modesty about one's person is important because it signifies respect. In acting with modesty and respecting the modesty of others, one is behaving with respect for one's higher nature and the higher nature of others. We are in a compact whereby we will not breach the modesty of others that others should not breach ours. It suggests that there are certain aspects of one's being which are precious, intimate and private, and therefore not to be shamelessly exposed and flaunted. We do, of course, know that with us humans sexual love provokes the strongest and most intimate feelings and also the strongest sense of betrayal, which is part of the reason for surrounding the erotic with conventions of modesty and restraint.

It is also true that in the absence of these conventions a true sense of the erotic, and what it can offer our fallen state by way of consolation, becomes virtually unattainable, though that is not the reason for the conventions. The sort of shameless debauch which is now taken for granted among some sections of the population is a sad attempt to achieve the truly erotic, but it is bound to fail because it wipes away the conditions of restraint, mystery and intimate self-giving and self-disclosure which make the erotic possible. It is the difference between the so-called club scene in London or Leeds today and a formal and chaperoned ball in Bath in the eighteenth century. This difference might seem liberating on the surface, but it explains why you will not find a Mr Darcy in the Ministry of Sound or the Majestik, because the whole point of the club of today is to eradicate the sensibility and degree of formality needed to produce Mr Darcy.

In essence, feeling shame is an integral part of having standards. If you do not have a propensity to feel shame and do not actually feel shame on occasion, it is hard to see what having standards amounts to. We can, naturally, argue about the worth or otherwise of particular standards. No doubt today, for all sorts of reasons, we feel comfortably superior to the Conradian hero who insists on dressing for dinner in the Congo, surrounded only by half naked savages (as he, but not we would see it). Nor do we feel that shame should attach any longer to illegitimacy, for it is unfortunate if children are stigmatised for their parents' failings, and in this case it may be hard

171

to punish the parents without opprobrium attaching to the children. Standards certainly change over the years, and when this happens it is often perceived, rightly or wrongly, as decline and the onset of shamelessness.

But while some may regard it as a good thing that we are more shameless in all sorts of ways than our grand-parents, we need to ask ourselves whether absence of shame in such matters as scrounging, personal dishonesty, cowardice, infidelity, insobriety, immodesty, bad manners and laziness is a sign of a well ordered society. There are not impossible ideals, shame in regard to which will inevitably produce mental breakdown, but merely the staples of an orderly life. One wonders whether someone continually subject to these vices should not, on occasion, have doubts about his or her self-esteem.

I have no doubt that many of those who dismiss shame and who say that we should as a society relax our standards so as to make it less likely that people will feel shame decry the violence, the boorishness and the sheer disorder which is so prevalent a feature of contemporary urban life. They will also decry of the irresponsibility and drug abuse rife among large swathes of the young, par-ticularly young men. But what they need to ask themselves is whether you can have even a modicum of civility in a society without a balancing modicum of shame. They should also ask themselves whether the real repression of heavy policing and illiberal laws on which the Government appears set may not be worse than the supposed repression of children being brought up to feel ashamed when they have failed in some basic moral demand.

In fact the latter sort of repression is not really repression at all. Neither is it a curb on our freedom, except in the morally inverted world of contemporary psychotherapeutic theory. It is rather the way in which each of us has to begin to free ourselves from the tyranny of ungoverned instinct, a tyranny to which the shameless are condemned to be subjected, as many in their anger and despair at their condition recognise deep down, albeit inchoately and inarticulately. Shame and the potential for feeling it on the appropriate occasion, far from being incompatible with freedom and self-esteem, is actually the condition of both.

11

INTERNET

Common to all the aspects of the contemporary cave which we have considered has been displacement of reality. But as significant as any, and symbolic of much else in our life, is the much vaunted, though ill-named concept of virtual reality (virtual reality being neither real nor virtuous).

For the world of virtual reality is one composed of pixels on screens. But by means of these pixels, one can simulate whatever fantasy one wishes, all without the pain or effort of dealing with anything real.

The experience machine is a philosophical myth, albeit instructive. But there is nothing mythical about the people who spend much of their leisure time playing computer games, in which they simulate all kinds of experiences and adventures. Nor is there anything mythical about the growth of internet pornography, an endless source of solitary sexual fantasy. Nor is there anything mythical about internet chat rooms, in which, in sordid isolation self-invented personae engage in simulated communication with other self-invented personae. And there are even internet religious sites—pagan as well as Christian—whose virtue, according to their advocates, is that one can gain spiritual solace from them without the trouble or embarrassment of entering a place of worship or publicly admitting to one's faith.

A few years ago there was a cartoon of a university lecturer who, in the first picture, instead of lecturing live to his students, gave them a tape to listen to. In the second, the students have all gone, replaced themselves by tape recorders recording the master tape. That was funny then. But no more. The government, in order to make up for the lack of good teachers, is actively promoting the idea of internet classrooms, in which lessons given by expert teachers will be sent through cyberspace to pupils sitting at computer screens. Meanwhile a scheme based in Oxford, with an editorial board of Oxford dons, has been set up in which lectures by a group of 'some of the world's greatest academics' will be sold as internet packages.

Anyone with any sense of the human meaning of education will be instinctively repelled by these initiatives. But we should be careful to see what is wrong with them. Their defenders (who tend to be also their salesmen) will say that there is nothing essentially different about these proposals from telling a student to read a book. And it is true that Plato himself represents Socrates as objecting to the invention of writing, on the grounds that it would encourage men to rely on external marks rather than take what they learn into their souls and making it a part of themselves.

There are, of course, modern educators who would take externalism of this sort as a virtue. What matters, they say, is not what you know, but whether you have the ability to find things out, to pinball around the internet as one puts it, or, in an earlier version, invest in the Encyclopedia Britannica.

Both proposals are equally crass, for without a good base of knowledge you will not appreciate the significance of what you read or see; even less will you be able to sift the wheat from the chaff on the internet. No one who sees the internet as the future foundation for education seems to take seriously the fact that its very openness means that it is the greatest repository ever devised for cranks, charlatans, conspiracy theorists, obsessives and the plain ignorant, who would not otherwise be able to publicise their views. For the uneducated a degree of censorship in textbooks and a few hurdles to publication of pet theories are actually highly beneficial.

But, important as all this is, it does not get to the heart of the matter. Let us suppose that these lectures were all by the likes of Niall Ferguson, Steven Pinker, Richard Dawkins, Martin Rees and Daniel Dennett, and which might thereby be guaranteed to have some standing and credibility. Downloading this stuff could not in itself be an education, as people from Oxford above all should appreciate. A virtual university could not be a university, properly speaking.

For the key to a proper undergraduate education—in Oxford anyway—is not the lecture or even the book. It is the tutorial, and with good reason. For in the tutorial the student articulates what he or she has assimilated through lectures, books, and, even if you like, films and e-lectures, and his or her reactions to what has been assimilated, and tries out what he or she has got against the experience of the tutor.

Education is not just the acquisition of knowledge, though it cannot proceed without the acquisition of knowledge. It is, as Michael Oakeshott has put it, an initiation into the skill and partnership of the human conversation begun millennia ago 'in the primeval forests and extended and made more articulate in the course of centuries'. This is why true education both requires that we know what has gone on in that conversation up to now, and also why being lectured at by a domineering star of the podium or even of the television or internet screen is not necessarily the best way of working one's way falteringly into the conversation.

Why, though, would a chat-room tutorial not be as good as meeting one's tutor in the flesh? What does mere bodily presence add to an encounter of minds in cyber-space? The answer has to do with the responsibility of real encounter.

In a real encounter, one might indeed act a role, not just in the sense that one is performing a role, but in the more insidious sense that one is performing a role one does not really, in one's heart, believe in. So one can distinguish between a politician who acts differently in giving a speech from how he is when is with his family, but who nevertheless believes in the speech he is giving, from one who gives the same speech with full dramatic force, but who does not actually, in his heart, believe in what he is advocating.

The second politician is a hollow man. One suspects—and hopes—that his hollowness will be revealed as he has to face and deal with people who may be depending on his sincerity. Indeed his own insincerity will be brought home to him more vividly than perhaps he himself initially realised, as he actually encounters these people, who will be hanging on his words and deeds in all sorts of situations, more or less critical.

Education in the academic sense is not precisely like practicing politics. Nevertheless, if education is to go beyond a merely superficial acquisition of facts, opinions and mannerisms, one would expect it to be a part of one's personal development. This is what is right with Plato's complaint about writing. What is wrong with that complaint is that, far from impeding one's personal development, the study of texts actually allows one to muse on those texts, to work on them, to ingest their meaning and to criticise them in a far deeper way than if one simply had them stored in fleeting, evanescent form in one's memory. One is not able to lay before one's eyes and mind in permanent and objective form so as to be fit for systematic study and reflection texts which are merely spoken or called up in memory or, even less, images which flash by on screens. So having written texts before one is a key element in the personal journey we want education to be.

But so also is encounter with a teacher and with other students. Only in such encounters can one really test out one's reactions to what one is studying or even whether one has really understood or remembered it. We have all had the experience of reading something by which we are initially utterly convinced—only to have this conviction eroded, and often rightly eroded, when we have to express what we have been convinced by to our peers or betters. And part of what is involved in what Leavis used to call a 'collaborative-creative process' of this sort is one's own personal engagement and identification with what one is proposing. Is it I who am staking myself with this view and identifying with it, I, the whole person, and not just a virtual, irresponsible and disembodied phantasm communicating via e-mail with some other equally disembodied phantasm.

Postal and e-mail tutorials may be better than no education at all, but they can at best be substitutes for meetings between real teachers and real students. Some may find it moot, whether it might not be better to get an e-mail from a telegenic Pinker or a charismatic Dawkins (assuming, which does not actually seem to be the case, that this might be part of what the grandees are intending) rather than meeting dull old Dr Smith of Balls Pond Road University. But assuming that Smith has any knowledge or life in him at all, once the initial pleasure in being noticed by the grandee is over, there is really no comparison.

Even if a student receives as detailed written comments as could be imagined on an essay (a big if, in most cases, one suspects), that is only the start: the student also needs to be able to discuss those comments with the tutor in the light of his or her actual state of understanding, and the tutor needs to be able to expand and qualify what has been written in the light of the student's living reactions. Nor, for similar reasons, is there any substitute in education for building up some sort of real relationship with a real tutor. And, apart from formal encounters with one's teachers, there is no substitute in education at any level for informal encounters with one's peers, in which young people explore together all kinds of questions, cultural, scientific, moral, political and personal, both connected and unconnected with their formal studies.

On-line schooling and e-lectures may not do much good. But if they are not regarded as a substitute for proper teaching and learning, they may no do much harm either, provided they do not encourage us to start taking the e-world for reality. Danger starts when we begin to take the world of fantasy, play and wish-fulfilment for reality, when the costlessness of virtual reality takes over from the hard tests proferred by dealing with other people, real things and standards outside ourselves which matter. Dangers of this sort are all too present in on-line religion, on-line relationships and on-line pornography. In all three cases, we are dealing with the strongest of feelings and emotions. Full personal engagement and identification is of the essence, and giving free play to one's delusions and fantasies is likely to be utterly destructive both of oneself and also, when one re-enters the real world, of those around one.

As far as religion goes, we are only too familiar with the insidious effects of inward-looking and self-enclosed cults. All that militates against these effects is the entry of a cult and its adherents into the public world, where the beliefs and practices of the cult will be brought up against normal life and expectations, and often modified as a result. But even real-life encounters between one's private faith and the public world are not always enough to prevent extreme psychological pressure and worse on initiates into cults. The danger of highly-charged psychological domination in the service of some extreme sect is surely even greater in a 'virtual' cult. The very advantage supporters of on-line religion claim for it—its privacy— is in fact its greatest danger; for within the intimacy and privacy of the internet all kinds of obsessions and fantasies can flourish unchecked.

Much the same is true of internet and chat-room relationships. It is true that in real-life, face to face relationships people may chose to conceal aspects of their lives and personalities, with greater or less success. But in chat rooms, it is not what people chose to conceal about themselves, but rather what they chose selectively to reveal—often mixed with a high degree of deception, fantasy and lying. Apart from the inherent harm of such deceptions in themselves, such an approach to relationships can hardly be a healthy preparation for real-life encounters, which depend both on a degree of truth and on a degree of coming to terms with the recalcitrance of reality.

Nor does it seem entirely fanciful to question the effect on people's minds of the hours spent on computer games. Addictive in themselves, if played to any great extent, these games are a potentially lethal cocktail of the solitary and the imaginary. They involve an invented reality, whose danger is that to the adherents it can often seem more real, and certainly more exciting, than true reality. They substitute for everyday life all kinds of weird realms and fantasies, controlled it is true, but controlled by an uncontrolled imagination rather than by normality. For open and social encounters with real people, they substitute imagined encounters with unreal people. Locked into solitary fantasy, and the unreal excitements dreamed up therein, the gamer disqualifies himself for dealing with real life and real people. In these games one can exist and act in all kinds of different forms, without being inconvenienced by the demands or checks of everyday life, but also without appreciating its consolations and gifts.

And this brings us on to what is reliably claimed to be

the biggest traffic on the internet: pornography. Pornography may not always and in all circumstances be harmful, and maybe it even has its uses in genuine relationships. However, as a substitute for genuine relationships it is certainly harmful, as Philip Larkin revealed, perhaps inadvertently, in the famous witticism quoted earlier on the subject of masturbation. In pornography we are characteristically presented with perfect images of perfect bodies, perfectly compliant, all of which features are present to a high degree on internet porn, which is also available at whim, completely privately and, we are told, interactive. Users of it report on its addictive nature, but worse perhaps is the way its easy satisfaction and apparent perfection makes people less prepared to put up with the surface imperfections of real people and with the difficulties and obstacles of real relationships.

But this acceptance of the apparently easy and perfect is itself an illusion. Not only does it encourage people to avoid the hard work of real life and make them dissatisfied with the inevitable blemishes of life, but it is ultimately dissatisfying itself. It is in this sense that pornography can become addictive; in itself unsatisfactory it simply feeds the appetite for more—and for more dissatisfaction.

In fact, of course, the consolations which are to be gained from real relationships come precisely through working through difficulty and stress, and from the real achievements of living together and, if one is lucky, of bringing up one's children.

12

SPORT

In 1899 in his sardonic treatise *The Theory of the Leisure Class*, the economist Thorstein Veblen argued that any wealth which goes beyond what is needed for survival requires display for its own sake. The leisure class are those people in any society who have more than they actually need, and this surplus produces leisure. In the forms of display leisure makes possible, the more useless the better, for its purpose of such display was simply to show one's wealth and status off. The sheer excess one is striving to demonstrate would be compromised were any usefulness bound in with the display.

In this thesis, Veblen is doubtless echoing the moralism of Rousseau, who saw the arts and sciences of civilised life as little more than expressions of vanity, what he referred to as amour-propre, the desire to show oneself superior to others. For Veblen all, and for Rousseau much, of what counted as high culture was worthless display. This worthless display Veblen called conspicuous consumption.

In a characteristic and thought-provoking passage, Veblen speaks of the purchase of an article of consumption by a purchaser who is not an expert judge of materials or workmanship: 'He makes his estimate of the value of the article chiefly on the ground of the apparent expensiveness of the finish of those decorative parts and features which have no immediate relation to the intrinsic usefulness of the article; the presumption being that some sort of ill-defined proportion subsists between the substantial value of the article and the expense of the adornment added in order to sell it.'

Veblen wanted to extend this thought to high culture in general, and particularly to the study of the dead languages of southern Europe, as he puts it (which does not stop him from quoting from Latin, one of those languages, to good effect). To his mind the classics are merely further objects of conspicuous consumption. While he is surely wrong about the worth of the classics, what he says seems to characterise perfectly the present day manifestations of the cave and its fantasies—designer clothes, pop music, television, contemporary celebrity and the like. Being quite worthless in themselves, they are prime vehicles for conspicuous consumption.

The meaninglessness of our fantasies and their frenetic frothiness is rooted in their unreality. Disconnected from anything other than themselves, there is no way of judging these illusions except in relation to themselves, as images flung on the wall of our cave. More deeply, we can come to suspect that a world constructed to conform to human desire—rather than the other way round—is going to share the same insubstantiality and potential for unease as the images of our time.

Interestingly and presciently Veblen, writing in 1899, thought that modern society had stumbled across an even better vehicle for leisured display than the study of the classics: 'Athletics has an obvious advantage over the classics for the purpose of leisure class learning, since success as an athlete presumes, not only a waste of time, but also a waste of money, as well as the possession of certain highly unindustrial archaic traits of character and temperament.'

Veblen is right about the exponential growth of sport in the twentieth century, and beyond, and he is also right to connect it to waste of money. Sport is obviously now one of the key areas of expenditure and leisure, and in many ways it is an adjunct of the worlds of media and celebrity. Celebrities ingratiate themselves with sportsmen and vice versa, and both are feasted on by the media. But, however industrially useless sports are—and Veblen is right to draw our attention to that, too—and however much sport provides images for the prisoners to gaze at on the wall of the cave, there is one aspect of sport which sets it apart from other cave fantasies.

It is that in sport there is a strong injection of reality. Someone has to win and some have to lose. Winning and losing are objective matters, however trivial, corrupt, spiteful or uninspiring the sport.

Furthermore, although all kinds of training and

preparation are allowed in sport, one thing which is almost universally excoriated is the use of performance enhancing drugs. It is interesting to examine the reason behind this prejudice, which, despite its deep-rootedness, can be made to seem irrational. For, it would be argued, all kinds of physical and mental training schemes, including special diets and supplements, are permitted to enhance performance, so why not drugs?

The feeling is that with drugs, some barrier delimiting the natural from the artificial has been crossed. Whereas ordinary or even extraordinary physical regimes and diets can be seen as supplementing the athlete's own capabilities and also as depending on his or her own work and dedication, with drugs we seem to be introducing something artificial from outside. This something has its effect without any effort on the part of the athlete, beyond that of actually taking the drug. Also even though we are familiar with the increased chances of the early onset of arthritis and heart conditions with some forms of training, the effects of drugs on athletes can be far more sudden and unpredictable.

In short, the use of drugs in sport offends the basic intuition we all have. Success in sport should be due to the athlete's own basic skill and aptitude, and what he or she has built on that initial natural endowment by his or her own efforts and fitness regimes. The achievement of even the most highly coached and fanatically fit athlete is real in a way drug induced performances are not.

This is highly significant, and not just for sport. For it

188

demonstrates the prejudice we all still have in favour of our achievements and successes taking place in the context of a reality which is not totally malleable and which cannot be dictated by us. Nevertheless, despite an element of honesty and even of elitism central to it, sport is a thoroughly compromised activity, a major part indeed of the fantasy world of the Cave, and for millions of us— who do not actually participate—not much more than that. The professionalisation of sport has gone hand in hand with increased standards of achievement, though not of sportsmanship.

Football, the self-styled 'beautiful game' is nothing of the sort. As a spectacle it is marred by cheating, violence and all manner of spitefulness. Its crowds behave appallingly, in contrast to the crowds which follow rugby, a far more violent, but in the end a far more honest game. Off the field football players, the English ones anyway, behave as appallingly as the game's followers would had they the incomes of the players. And the directors and managers who run football at the top level are collectively an astonishing crew, whose behaviour is often arbitrary and unpredictable in ways which one imagines would not be tolerated in other areas of business.

All this is, of course, because of the money which television has poured into the game, in effect taking it over. Television dictates even the timings of football of matches (even down to the precise moment the referee in a televised match blows the kick-off whistle), so as to ensure that not a night passes without some 'live' match being available to the viewer. It promotes the game and its celebrities remorselessly, in a manner reminiscent of the Roman emperors giving a pliant populace their bread and circuses. And politicians, ever anxious to establish their populist and proletarian credentials, cling to game's coat-tails as if they were effete Roman senators carefully ensuring their visibility at the Collosseum they in their hearts despised.

In England's winning of the rugby world cup in 2003, we were given perhaps a final inkling of how sport once was, how it should be, and how it will probably never be again. Rugby is a hard game, a game of great courage and, appearances notwithstanding, of great skill and intelligence too. It is a cliché, but in rugby no quarter is given—at any level—and none asked. Perhaps because of that there is an unspoken code of acceptable behaviour in rugby which, though frequently pushed to the limit, is rarely actually breached, and which when breached brings down universal condemnation from all involved (as happened notoriously in the England—South Africa match in November 2002, and from which South African rugby took some time to emerge). If this code were commonly breached, the game would become murderous, and the players recognise that. After the game, still, players who had been dishing it out to each other on the field in the most extreme way consistent or just about consistent with the code, fraternise. Lifelong friendships are born of such rivalry. In its essence, rugby is a club game, with its roots in communities. And it is also a team game in which, genuinely, success requires all for one and one for all.

All of this, and all this spirit, was evident in the 2003 world cup, and in the England team which won it. Though highly professional in approach and preparation, this team consisted of players who had been brought up in the earlier ethos which still exists in the game, in their clubs and in their own play. Part of the huge response to their victory was a recognition in the country of the nature of the team and of their game, a response which was echoed in the amazing and amazingly peaceful and unthreatening reception of the victors in London by over 750,000 English flag waving enthusiasts, a startling manifestation of political incorrectness which the authorities hardly knew how to handle. In an era dominated by the 'beautiful game', people instinctively looked back to a more beautiful time. They warmed to the startling honesty of the play of the likes of Martin Johnson, Jonny Wilkinson and Neil Back and their equally startling embarrassment at the celebrity foisted on them. Showcasing their personalities as celebrities was the very last thing they were doing or thinking of doing.

But make no mistake. This was a magnificent anachronism. Within days of the rugby world cup the papers were back to ten pages of coverage of our second class football for every page of rugby. The acres and hours of football coverage in the press and on radio and television continued unabated, to be consumed passively by the fans, the vast majority of whom do not play football themselves. Although football, like other sports, does have a sense of objective winning and losing and also a hierarchy of talent and success, which may seem to distance it from the fantasies of the Cave, from another point of view of its spectators it is yet another fantasy on the wall of the cave. It appeals as passively as one might like to the lowest common denominator. It is something accessible to all. And, as we see with David Beckham and many others, it merges seamlessly into the vapid world of celebrity. To the extent that sports aspire to the media driven and media sated condition of football, they will be similarly divorced from any grounding in reality.

13

NATURE

It is not through spectator sport and its attendant media circus that we might emerge from the fantasies of the Cave. If we wish to regain contact with reality, we might begin by looking rather to the exponential growth in sports in which the individual pits him or herself against the forces of nature, be they mountains, rocks, snow, rivers, oceans, deserts, Arctic tundra, caves, or the air itself as a medium to fall or glide through.

'The ubiquitous laws, the rules, the codes, the systems, the standardisation of our society stifles us, and every day deprives us of more and more responsibility. The desire to let all this go and to find ourselves face to face takes hold, and in the thousand and one ways which are available to us—even though they might be fatal—to let the reasons for being appear, so as to reveal to us the value of life, the value of our existence.' Thus (in my translation) Dominique Perret, *extrême skieur extraordinaire*.

In contrast to our Cave induced fantasies, there is

something challenging, indestructible and remorseless about the powers of nature, and something heroic, if in the end futile, about those who test themselves against them. Perret continues: 'In the mountains there are many dangers. There are formidable ones and there are initially trivial ones which can't always be overcome face to face, in one go. We have to transform them, turning them from 'enemies' into 'friends'. In modifying the game, you can circumvent obstacles; you can turn the 'no' of failure into victory… When I return to-morrow or the day after, I will perhaps have better luck or better knowledge on my side. But one thing is certain whatever happens. The mountain itself will not have moved. It will still be there for fresh adventures.'

In the end the mountains always win. Climbers die— even the best of them, and in uncomfortably large numbers as readers of Joe Simpson and Jim Wickwire will be well aware—or, if they are lucky, they retire, as do most skiers, but the mountains remain. Still, in pitting oneself against a mountain, one may also adapt to its demands, and so for a time come to make it a friend, as Perret suggests. But the friendly mountain is the one you have been able to adapt to—not, as with the fantasies of the Cave, the other way around. As anyone who has been on even a small mountain in a gale or a fog or a whiteout will know, mountains do not adapt to human beings. You fall off them, or in the case of snow and ice you fall through them, the wind blows you backwards, an avalanche blows you away and smothers you, you completely lose your bearings on them. All this and worse can happen, often without warning, even after the most benign possible start. Even in the best of conditions there is always a moment when you realise that it is just you, confronted with the immensity and sheer facticity of the mountain, in all its inscrutable, stony detail, as well as in its sombre grandeur and pristine purity; and, of course, never far from consciousness, there is the ever present possibility of death, not of death in general, but of one's own death, now, soon, a bit later.

In Wordsworth's terms, our sensibility is here 'fostered alike by Beauty and by fear'. Everything else is wiped away in the intensity of the action, and in the confrontation with a reality, by turns lowering, alien and, in the eighteenth century sense, sublime—except that when one is on the mountain, sublimity is not a matter of disinterestedly savouring the sensation of an overpowering force. It is a mater of very interestedly savouring it, with Beauty not untinged by fear and by other darker aspects of the aesthetics of nature. Adapting to a mountain is no easy settling onto a comfortable ledge, adapted to our shapes and needs; it should involve the utmost of physical strength and mental concentration, but strength and concentration working with the mountain's impersonal force rather than against it—and even that will be unavailing against unpredictable changes in wind or weather.

What I have said about mountains will also apply, parri passu, to the sea, to caves, to the air, to deserts, to polar regions, and to all those dimensions of nature people want to explore in ever more extreme fashion, and to test themselves against. Even those who do not adventure into the wild themselves, or who have never attempted to do so, respond favourably to the exploits of those who do, far more favourably than we do to the media celebrities, politicians and footballers whose doings occupy so much of the public's consciousness.

All this raises the question as to why it should be so. Why is it that nature so impresses us? One might be reminded of Mallory's reason for wanting to climb Everest: 'Because it is there.' Well, it might be said, lots of things are there, but we don't necessarily want to visit them.

Nevertheless there is something important in what Mallory said. It is the sheer and overwhelming thereness of the mountains and other natural phenomena, which fascinates us. It makes them attractive in just the way the more flaky and insubstantial manifestations of human civilisation are not, and which, for those in touch with them, can even come to endow them with personality, as Wordsworth has it in 'The Prelude':

> The grim shape
> Towered up between me and the stars, and still,
> For so it seemed, with purpose of its own
> And measured motion like a living thing,
> Strode after me...
> No familiar shapes

Remained, no pleasant images of trees,
Of sea, or sky, no colours of green fields;
But huge and mighty forms, that do not live
Like living men, moved slowly through the mind
By day, and were a trouble to my dreams.

For some there may be a question as to whether Wordsworthian piety towards nature becomes a form of idolatry, of nature-worship. Certainly there is such a thing as nature worship in which natural objects are treated as if, in their inanimate form, they were divine beings. Less idolatrous, but still problematic, is seeing natural forces and objects—the wind, trees, etc—as the expressions of divine beings, their abodes, or even their incarnate forms. This is problematic because we know (do we not?) that natural forces and objects are subject to natural laws. They do not operate under the dictates of gods or spirits, even less are they in control of their own destinies, as they might be if they were in any straight-forward sense the visible manifestations of divinities. What, though, is not so clearly ridiculous would be to see nature both as a whole, and in all its multifarious detail, as the expression of a divine force or spirit.

In this context, the regularities of nature, so much emphasised in modern science, would themselves be an expression of the divine force. This was, indeed, how it was seen by Newton. For Newton and for many of his contemporaries, nature's very mechanism, in its simplicity, in its universal extent, and in its apparent exceptionlessness was an indication of the divinity. But it was, perhaps, an impersonal, remote divinity, which quickly dropped out of focus as the mechanism appeared the more complete in its scope, and utterly self-regulating and self-sustaining to boot, so the less in need of any divine intervention or support. Even if in the mists of time a god had started it all, its current operations could be entirely explained by the laws Newton and his successors discovered.

In practice, however, Newtonian mechanisms cannot explain everything. There is much in our world that cannot actually be explained in terms of the operation of inert matter. Life itself brings other types of activity and potentiality into play than are revealed in models of atoms and the void. Such things as self-replication, cellular development and splitting, and the metabolism and striving of organisms, even the simplest, are all man-ifestations of a type of existence not foreshadowed in the study of the inorganic.

Within the living world conscious experience takes us into yet another dimension, though no doubt one foreshadowed in the tendency of living things to react to their circumstances (as opposed to merely being acted on and pushed around by them). To those sensitive to the complexity of nature, and to the emergence of different types of existence in response to different circumstances, the Newtonian vision of the world consisting of no more than inert particles moving in a colourless, silent, intangible void will come to seem less and less

compelling. And in this appreciation of the creative possibilities of nature, we might begin to think—against
Newton—that divinity is revealed not so much in the
regularity of the universe as in its irregularities which
permit the emergence of new and unsuspected levels of
action and reaction.

Seeing the world as itself a process replete with possibilities of creative development will go hand in hand
with a sense that reality is greater than us and within
which our own lives are enclosed. This sense of our lives
being rounded by a reality which encloses us and sustains
us will be reinforced if we regard the creative potential
of the world as itself the manifestation of an intelligence
and will intimately involved in the process. We will begin
to look on the world as something within which
humanity has a rightful place and significance, rather
than as a context inert and irresponsive to life and intelligence, simply there for us to dispose of in accordance
with whatever desires we happen to have. Seeing the
world as replete with vital possibility will also feed back
into our attitude to what we had initially regarded as
brute matter; after all, even if the universe began with
simple atoms of hydrogen and helium, those simple
atoms must have had the potential for biological and
intelligent developments. They may not ever have been
as 'simple' or inert as we might be inclined to think from
a Newtonian or classical atomist perspective.

The physical universe is, of course, a deeply
ambiguous phenomenon. Some of the differences are

neatly symbolised by the philosophical writings of two distinguished French biologists, both, as it happens, Nobel prize winners. On the one hand there is the late Jacques Monod, author of *Chance and Necessity* (New York, 1971). According to Monod, the universe is a combination of deterministic laws at the level of physics, and of wholly random events at the biological level. Life and all its manifestations are simply chance happenings within a coldly deterministic setting. There is no sense in which the universe aims at life or consciousness or intelligence or anything else. Our existence is simply a matter of myriads of chance events, any one of which might have been different, and which would have led to quite different outcomes, and ultimately to quite different world histories. We are momentary specks of mentality in an environment which cares nothing for us, and which has done nothing to prepare for us. We and other conscious and living beings exist, but there is no sense in which we, or creatures like us had to exist.

On the other hand, there is Christian de Duve, author of *Vital Dust* (New York, 1995). De Duve does not deny that, at a certain level, biological development is due to random processes. Precise outcomes in the biological realm are not predictable. However, recognising the role of randomness in microcosmic happenings is not inconsistent with there being quite predictable tendencies at the macroscopic level. Given the immense numbers of biological mutations, and combining that with the very small number which are actually going to succeed in any environment and with the quite strict morphological constraints on actual biological development, we can say fairly safely that given an environment in which, say, sight is favourable, sight will occur, and through the use of light-sensitive cells. Indeed, as if in vindication of this line of thought, it is claimed that sight of this sort has emerged in evolutionary history on at least 40 separate and unconnected occasions.

For de Duve, though not for Monod, it is no mystery that large numbers of biological developments have happened more than once. Nor is it a mystery that complexity, carbon based life, and consciousness, intelligence and the rest, which were present in the original seeds of the universe, should have been actualised, maybe more than once. All these things have always been there, potentially, from the beginning, and there as the direction in which the universe and the beings in it are bound to tend. Hence 'vital dust'; and hence, too, de Duve's conviction that we are part of a universal process which will produce advances in all kinds of ways we can hardly suspect. It may well have produced life similar to ours many times over in our universe and in many different places.

The contrasting attitudes of Monod and de Duve may not be directly decidable on strictly scientific grounds. What each says is compatible with all the scientific evidence. Monod's attitude is a modern variant of the old view held by the Greek atomists, by the Roman philosopher-poet Lucretius and later by

Hume and Bertrand Russell. Basically we are no more than a random collection of particles, bound together for a short time so as to produce feeling and thought, and to struggle for survival and perhaps reproduction, in a cold, unfeeling and hostile universe, which, in our own environment, contains many creatures out to get us and do us down. Our only recourse is to survive in the struggle while we can and enjoy life while we can, before we inevitably dissolve back into the lifelessness of the infinite void. On this view, it is hard to see why we should have any feeling towards nature or indeed treat nature as more than a resource for our experience. If we could by-pass nature altogether, via Brave New World or some form of experience machine, so much the better.

To the extent, then, that we do have feelings towards nature and have respect for it, we are belying the Monod-Russell attitude, for on that view feeling towards nature are based on false beliefs, and respect for nature will be misplaced. Clearly anything approaching a Wordsworthian attitude will be completely primitive. If, on the other hand, nature is a creative process in which we are intimately involved, and in which even the smallest particles are not the inert and simple atoms of Newtonian myth, but are 'vital dust', complex and active things with potentiality for and drive towards complexity, including life and consciousness, then piety towards natural phenomena would be an intelligible response. And our more than instinctive reservations about completely artificial environments and our yearning for a raw, untouched nature would both be explicable and intelligible.

That so many of us do feel this way, and very strongly and despite all the efforts of educators and apologists of the Monod camp could and perhaps should be taken as some evidence that their view is a shallow one, overlooking real currents which flow between us and the rest of nature. Nature not only sustains us, but we are part of nature's creative process, based in the most basic properties of nature, and not—as the Monod-Russell view has it, a chance by-product of elements and forces with no propensity to life, consciousness or intelligence. In what we do we develop that process, for good or ill. Piety towards nature consists in recognising our genesis in nature, and a need to stay in touch with nature.

Without sharing Milton's theological vision, and even in a post-religious age, the archangel Raphael's words to Adam in 'Paradise Lost' can still resonate. Speaking of the expanse of the heavens, Raphael says

And for the Heaven's wide circuit, let it speak
The Maker's high magnificence, who built
So spacious, and his line stretched out so far,
That Man may know he dwells not in his own.

This sense of dwelling not in our own remains a strong antidote to the clamorous and Man produced illusions and fantasies of the Cave. But we should also remember that just before the passage quoted, Raphael has pointed out that

> The Earth
> Though, in comparison of heaven, so small,
> Nor glistering, may of solid good contain
> More plenty than the Sun that barren shines,
> Whose virtue on itself works no effect,
> But in the fruitful Earth; there first received,
> His beams, unactive else, their vigour find.

The balance to be sought is that of realising the uniqueness of human life in what we know of the universe, and how in what we know, with us alone in our experience brute matter becomes articulate, (the otherwise unactive beams finding their vigour in and through us), without forgetting that we dwell not in our own. Against nature conceived in this way, talk of 'self-esteem' and of celebrity is shown up for the triviality it is.

14

WORK

Tension there may be in our attitude to nature. It is at once greater than us and articulated through us, but there is no real contradiction. Indeed some of the same themes and sensibilities which are revealed in our attitudes to nature also show up in similarly deep rooted attitudes to work.

The phrase 'significant toil' is not a fashionable one. Nevertheless it does encapsulate certain widely held prejudices. Why do most of us feel that there is something amiss with an economy which, however rich in financial services, 'hospitality', access and media activity, does not actually produce anything physically? Why is farming (still, and all the caveats about agri-business notwithstanding) a more respected profession that advertising? Why is there something admirable about the Conradian sailor, doing his duty on many a watch, over and over again so repetitively, more admirable by far than a host of super-models or professional footballers? Why does a tailor, in say, Turkey, making clothes to last in timeless style seem inherently more worthy of respect than the celebrity designers whose 'creations' capture the media focus? Why is the Turner prize infinitely more meretricious, less honest, than the efforts of even the most plodding water-colourist painting in Richmond Park?

The answer to these questions can have nothing to do with economics. After all, economically an economy based on services may be far more successful than one based on production. Farming, particularly small farming, may show little return compared with advertising. Solid duties, like under-stated clothes and art of genuine technique and long training, are never going to be noticed in a world dominated by ephemeral media, ever hungry for sensation.

We are all very aware that we live in a world hungry for sensation, which the media feeds and on which it feeds, and we are also aware of the disposable nature of that world and of its products. That world, in contrast to the worlds of professions and crafts supported by long traditions of skill and artistry, has no standards except those it continually invents and re-invents for itself, in ever more frenetic spirals of hype and sensation. There is a feeling, too, that advertising, the media and services are parasitic activities, dependent on the real work of actually making things.

One is reminded here of one aspect of Hegel's famous discussion of the master and the slave. The master appears to be in the ascendant, but, says Hegel, that is only appearance, and appearance which will be wiped away once the true position is recognised particularly by the slave. The master, it is true, gets the profit of the slave's work because of his superior firepower, but in two crucial respects the master is actually the less independent of the two.

The first is that the master depends in all sorts of ways on the slave's work. So if the slave or slaves were bold enough to stop working for the master, the master would quickly fall into a state of need. But the second point is the more fundamental. Unlike the master, the slave acts on the world, not only changing things, but also imprinting his personality on the world. The slave objectifies himself, in Hegel's terminology, or as we might say, expresses his personality in things, while the master simply orders the slave around and receives things from him. Not only does the master depend on the skill and craftsmanship of the slave for display, but in making what is displayed the slave makes a physical difference to the world, and has the psychological benefit of getting outside his own inner self, of expressing that inner self outwardly and of impressing it on a resistant reality. In this process, in its discipline and the possibilities it affords, both reality and self are tempered.

Is any of this relevant to our world? Like the master, most of us are consumers of the work of others. In passive consumerist mode, like the master, we are all in a certain sense slaves to those who do and organise the producing, and slaves particularly to the mass media. If we feel weakened and diminished by this passivity, as many of us do, and if we feel resentful of our enslavement to the media stars and producers of images and ephemera, we have the solution in our own hands.

We can deprive the producers of the trivia of the oxygen of audience. We can turn them off—literally—and do things for ourselves. We can sing, dance, play, act; we can also make things physically, like Hegel's craftsman-slave. And considering the absolute banality of most of the productions of pop music and the mass media, there is no reason to suppose that things we do, make and play for ourselves would be any less good, objectively speaking. The standard of music and music performance in the average Victorian salon was infinitely superior to the efforts of today's pop musicians. (They, the earlier ones that is, will have been playing Parry and Stanford, and even Mendelssohn, Chopin and Brahms, and without electronic aids.) The fact that we tend not to free ourselves from the consumerism of the Cave is testament to the seductiveness of the illusions; but the fact that we still feel uneasy about our enthralment shows that enslavement is not total.

We need to consider the liberation which comes through work. For Hegel the work has to be work in which the worker can put something of his own spirit and personality. As Carlyle put it in a striking passage in *Sartor Resartus*, which illustrates perfectly the emptiness of performance considered apart from what is performed, and which points to the poignancy and inarticulacy of mere feeling without objective expressive correlative:

'a certain inarticulate Self-consciousness dwells dimly

in us; which only our works can render articulate and decisively discernible. Our Works are the mirror wherein the spirit first sees its natural lineaments. Hence, too, the folly of that impossible Precept, Know thyself; till it be translated into this partially possible one, Know what thou canst work at.'

One thinks here, naturally, of the work of craftsmen, and also of the Ruskinian attitude to the carvers and sculptors of the Gothic cathedrals. For Ruskin the medieval craftsmen were all individuals in their craft and in the frequent imperfection of their work, so what they did bore the mark of their individual personalities. Ruskin preferred the roughness of the Gothic to what he saw as the cold perfection of the classical temple, because roughness was an indication that the work had been that of an individual in all his and its imperfection. Both the Gothic cathedral and the classical temple were highly ordered, but (according to Ruskin) the ordering in the classical case ruled out individuality in its very perfection, while the Gothic left room for the untidiness of nature and the expression of the individual hand, mind and spirit.

We may feel that Ruskin idealises the freedom of the Gothic sculptors and denigrates the talents and individuality of classical and neo-classical artists, even as they sink their personalities in an art of sublime impersonality. Personality may seem a very little thing in comparison to the perfection of a well-executed Corinthian capital, and we should appreciate that the way the Gothic carver expressed his personality in his gargoyle is a very different thing from the pop star showcasing her personality. The carver's personality, if it appears at all, appears as transmuted and sublimed through both the stone and the tradition in which he worked, to say nothing of his service in the great and over-arching work of the cathedral. But, even while qualifying what he says about personality, other things Ruskin said about work are surely relevant. For Ruskin a labour in which the person as a whole is not at all engaged is an assault on the worker; in Ruskin's own words, in the division of labour found in modern industrial processes it is not, truly speaking, the labour that is divided; but the men: 'Divided into mere segments of men—broken into small fragments and crumbs of life; so that all the little piece of intelligence that is left in a man is not enough to make a pin, or a nail, but exhausts itself in making the point of a pin or the head of a nail.'

Against Ruskin's attack on perfection, one feels that someone carving a classical triglyph or executing an architrave or a cornice from a copybook would not be broken into small fragments, even if he judged the success of the work as much as its impersonality as by its personality. Skill, intelligence and judgement are all involved, and of a high order, even without the addition of an individualised gargoyle. The same sort of thing could be said of a good motor mechanic or plumber. But not perhaps of the myriads of people doing mindless and depersonalising work with IT, or in 'customer service' call centres, or in fast food establishments, or in many offices, private as well as public, where 'procedures' rather than judgement rule. Teaching itself is treated by politicians, inspectors and officials—and by far too many teachers too, it has to be said—as a matter of 'delivering' a centrally imposed curriculum and tests by means of centrally sourced interactive whiteboards and IT packages. The teacher whose vocation is, or should be, the most humane of all becomes no less a franchisee than the manager of a Macdonalds restaurant, and no more either.

An important element in significant toil is what Conrad calls backbone: the backbone shown by the superficially absurd accountant, the only white man half way up the Congo River, who still wore a high starched collar, white cuffs, a light alpaca jacket, snowy trousers, a clear necktie and varnished boots, not the sort of get up favoured by contemporary celebrities of the media. Conrad (or rather Marlow) comments that his appearance 'was certainly that of a hairdresser's dummy; but in the great demoralisation of the land he kept up his appearance. That's backbone. His starched collars and got-up shirt-fronts were achievements of character.'

Backbone is important for the reason Conrad gives. It is where true self esteem might be found, dependent on channelling one's initial feelings into acceptable and certain form. It is quite unlike today's 'self-esteem' which consists of letting one's unformed desires express themselves in any way one likes, the less disciplined the better, it often seems. But as all parents know, happiness will never be found in the infantility of undisciplined emotion. Backbone, like the toil it often accompanies, is a bulwark against demoralisation, against the relentless advance of the metaphorical jungle, which is not, of course, and was not taken by Conrad to be, confined to the geographical jungle. (For him Brussels, a whited sepulchure, was worse than the Congo.)

Like work itself, backbone is a way of making one's mark in the world and on the world, and also of asserting the presence in us of a spirit more than the bestial. And work of backbone need not be against nature or nature's grain.

One of the great triumphs of the English aesthetic is the English garden, the fruit of much work and the impress of much personality, but intentionally sculpted with nature rather than constraining nature with geometric regimen. It is indeed a beautiful and sophisticated elaboration of vital dust that we and it both are. The English garden could be a model for much of what we are saying, for no garden, English or otherwise, lasts for long without toil and backbone, significant toil and stiff backbone; yet in the direction of the effort the English garden can be seen as a supreme expression of piety towards nature rather than an assault on nature and its forms. And in significant toil mere words about quality and excellence are empty; real standards simply show themselves, and real discriminations of quality simply follow.

15

FIDELITY

As well as by a buried appreciation both of nature and of the need for toil, we may be brought back from the fantasies of the Cave by a sense of the multiple contingency of our lives. For our lives are contingent in all sorts of ways, starting with our very identity. Without denying our freedom, we cannot underestimate the extent to which who and what we are are factors outside our control, however much we may seek to hide this fact from ourselves.

We do not chose the circumstances of our birth, our parents, our relations, our upbringing, our schooling, the opportunities we are given, our locality, our country or our culture. We can build on all these things, and adapt them, but there always remains a sense in which our roots are deeper than adaptations, not least because we are usually unaware of them and take them for granted. They are the unspoken and hidden context in which everything we do makes sense, or fails to make sense.

Piety has been defined by the philosopher George

Santayana as respect for those conditions of human existence which are not of our own making. Piety would obviously include the type of respect for the natural world we have been advocating earlier. But it would extend to those aspects of our history and heritage on which all of us depend, and which none of us have done anything to bring about. This extended notion of piety covers aspects of our lives of human making, but not of our own making. As such it connects with the ancient Roman virtue of pietas.

The Romans practiced devotion to the gods of hearth and household, to the gods of the dead and of wayfarers, to one's ancestral gods and those of the state, and also to the spirits of field, river and grove. So, when Aeneas fled from Troy, he took with himself on to the open sea not just his father, his people and his son, but also his hearth gods and the greater gods (*Aeneid*, Book 3, line 12). The gods were transplanted into Italy, where they gave the Romans a sense of who they were, of what was fitting within the family, of the divine mission of the Romans to bring peace, justice and civilisation to the world, and also of the proper limits of human life and ambition. Such anyway was Virgil's myth, and it was one which resonated deeply with the Roman people and with their innate piety, the BBC's *Rome* notwithstanding.

Aeneas with his father on his back, his son led by his hand and the hearth gods alongside is a striking image of the fact that we are not weightless choosers, existing only in our own time. We come into the world laden with the past, from which we derive our identity. We leave it with our children resting on whatever we have done within it. And while we are in it we should think of ourselves as subject to the duties and taboos implicit in having and revering gods, in having a sense of the sacredness of things.

There is little doubt that modern life is impious. We are encouraged to think of ourselves as having no baggage from the past, as being free and weightless choosers, self-inventors and consumers. This ideology is preached at us from left and right in politics. But modern people, no less than the Romans, have a deep need for piety, and even if unconscious a yearning for it. It would be hard to make sense of the ecological movement otherwise, and hard otherwise to understand the resistance to globalisation. The more efficient the global economy the more poignant becomes the lament of individuals mourning the passing of local and hallowed custom.

In a memorable phrase, Wittgenstein said how small a thought it takes to fill a whole life. Part of what might be meant by this is that even the most banal thought, like 'I must get the ironing done', presupposes a whole background and context, cultural and personal, for it to have the sense it does. This is a culture in which ironing is (or is not) important, in which ironed clothes are required for some activities (which?), in which the technology of ironing in this way exists, in which I am the sort of person who conceives this as my duty (and what this says about my particular upbringing and character), and also about my particular immediate situation, that there is ironing to be done, and which bits need to be done now, etc., etc. Reflecting in this way makes it easily possible to see how a whole life and culture condenses into the most trivial thought. It is less easy perhaps, when we are taken up by the weightless fantasies of the cave, to see how this 'whole life and culture' which sustains even our most trivial thoughts is both there, always, and contingent and outside our choosing. It could have been different—other people's forms of life are different—and it having formed me is not something I can alter, not can I wipe it away wholesale.

One of the illusions of the Cave and its associated phenomena is that we and our lives are wholly malleable, and can be changed at will, according to what images are thrown on the wall. It is a major premise of a certain type of market capitalism that we can become what we want, that through consumption of brands we can refashion our image and identity. But a similar notion is shared by New Labour and its theorists such as the sociologist Anthony Giddens, that in the modern world we are what we choose. Capitalists and New Labourites alike concur in thinking that we can in effect forget our heritage and the duties tradition and family impose on us, forging new identities at will.

All this emphasis on the weightless invidividual choser, from whatever political side, overlooks the point that even in the experience machine there is the experiencer, and the experiencer could not actually have the same thoughts as us—even about ironing—unless he shared the same form of life as us. Outside the form of life, the same words or thought ('I must get the ironing done') will have a wholly different sense.

Realising this fact may not lead us to cherish our form of life. No form of life should be cherished in every detail, any more than nature itself, and there are large swathes of our lives (and even of nature) which should not be cherished. But realising the extent to which I am formed by historical and cultural realities will make me realise at least that changing a form of life is neither going to be easy or cost free. It will certainly make me aware of the particularities and densities of particular cultures and histories, and have less of a touristic attitude to them, appreciating that different forms of life incarnate differences deeper and more thorough-going than those of surface appearance. It may also make me more respectful than I might otherwise be of my own inerited form of life, and also of its beneficent aspects and of the efforts of my ancestors in promoting and producing those beneficent aspects. Above all, reflection on the life in a thought should serve as an antidote to the ineffable presentism of the Cave: the fantasy that the present is all that there is, and that the present as projected in the Cave is reproducible across the globe.

Many of the complaints about globalisation are ill-judged and based on the economics of the kindergarten (roughly the idea that giving poor people jobs, opportunities and incomes they would not otherwise have is in itself exploitation). But complaint about the destruction of cultural roots implied in the spreading across the whole world of the culture of the Cave is justified, and it follows from a profounder grasp of human reality than is to be found in the world of the Cave. Nor is this a politically neutral point. For we find the same cast of thought in much of the advocacy of mass migration, which all too easily seems to those at the sharp end of immigration to be tantamount to telling them that it really does not matter whether or not their form of life continues in recognisable form and in a reasonably organic state of development.

Indeed in some cases, that is just what the advocates of mass migration are intending to tell them, because of their own prejudices against the nation states and national forms of Europe (though not, strangely, manifesting similar prejudice against traditional ways outside Europe). That the response of some at the sharp end of mass immigration is unjustifiable and even at best crudely articulated does not show that their case is unjustifiable. It may well rest on a profounder understanding of the reality of human life than the fashionable hostility to indigenous life and culture which masquerades under the guise of 'multi-culturalism'. Multi-culturalism can actually be a wedge for undermining host cultures in Europe, so much so that we now hear of British citizens speaking and thinking of their British passport as a 'travel document' conferring rights, but no duties or loyalty (which in their case may well be elsewhere).

That many of the anti-globalists would also be, in that sense, 'multi-culturalists' is no doubt a delightful paradox, though that would be of little consolation to those whose ways of life are so casually dismissed by the guardians of the Cave, who regard forms of life as little more than fashion accessories, to be put on or taken off at will. *Pietas* towards the past and tradition plays no role in this type of thinking, but the thinking is itself predicated on a shallow understanding of what it is to have an identity, that identity itself is just what cannot be chosen.

Over and above suggesting the way in which a life is condensed in a thought, Wittgenstein's words point to the way in which for a life to be filled, one does not need to travel far. All one needs is a thought which takes one deep. A man, he says, can spend his life travelling round the same little country and think there is nothing outside it—the obvious inference we are meant to draw that he might be none the worse for it either. Following on from this, one might say that contemporary life, the life of the Cave, is a life in which travel is regarded as an essential component of a good life, yet in travelling people learn nothing. They do not really learn about other cultures or even about their own. What they get are confused and superficial hints of local colour, as refracted through the fantasies current in the Cave and the conversations of one's equally ignorant companions. They rarely learn the languages of the places they visit or study their history.

Far from travel broadening the mind, most travel narrows it, as it confirms people in what they already believe, giving the illusion that their attitudes actually have some basis outside their own culture. Global tourism makes us all equally shallow.

But where, if not in gap years and their senior equivalents, should deep thoughts be sought? It may seem trite, moralistic even, to say, in the relationships to which one is committed, chosen and unchosen, and to emphasise that in distinction to the attitudes to relationships discussed earlier, even chosen relationships should often be regarded as involving an element of commitment.

To see relationships as involving commitments of various sorts, chosen and unchosen, is deeply antithetical to the spirit of the Cave, as we have seen, because it seems to put limits on the exercise of choice. Indeed it has become something of a dogma to think of relationships as essentially spontaneous, consisting of continually renewed undertakings, until renewability runs out and the parties move on to their next choice. We have already looked at the effect on children when their parents see themselves involved in continual and open-ended 'experiments in living', subject to cancellation or alteration at any time, unilaterally or bilaterally. But, important as this is, it is not the point I want to make here.

The point at issue here is the implicit tension between rootedness and disposability in a relationship. You may not like your roots, and you may reject much of what they amount to, on the surface at least, but for the reasons already elaborated you cannot avoid them. One thing which some people may not like about acknowledging their roots, personal, familial and cultural, is that thinking about oneself as rooted in these and other ways is at the same time to acknowledge multiple dependencies. Some find that this militates against their preferred self-image, as a free spirit, constructing one's own self and developing one's life as and when one wishes.

But this very desire, if taken too far, is itself an illusion and is doomed to failure. For, whatever the fantasies of the Cave might imply, we are not independent beings floating above what is. In all sorts of ways, often cruel, reality breaks in so as to demonstrate our dependence and what old fashioned moralists called the vanity of human wishes. Stoicism may be a response to the incursions of fate and the inevitable sickness, death and tragedy with which we are surrounded and which we will have to face, to say nothing of comparatively minor but no less hurtful problems like loss of job or reputation or the sheer bloody-mindedness and intractability of 'colleagues', partners and the rest. Stoicism may be a response, but it is a response few manage in practice as opposed to in theory. The thralls of sexuality, inevitable disappointment and failure professionally, illness, ageing, mortality are too deeply rooted in the lives of most of us to be simply thought away. And, even if managed, stoicism may not be the best way, as it may in practice be a fig leaf for to a lack of basic human feeling, where such feeling is called for, and called for properly.

The better and more human way may be to find—and give—support in one's relationships, chosen and unchosen. If at times we sense that the world which once seemed

> so various, so beautiful, so new,
> Hath really neither joy, nor love, nor light,
> Nor certitude, nor peace, nor help for pain.

Then, as Matthew Arnold said, on the darkling plain, where ignorant armies clash by night, there is just this left to us:

> Ah, love, let us be true
> To one another.

Trite this may sound in abstract, but it is actually a hard message. For what is being advocated here is a type of fidelity which is strong enough to survive all that has to be survived, and which in advance we may, perhaps thankfully, have no inkling of. Without fidelity, love, whether filial, marital, parental, companionate, pedagogical, regimental, religious or of any other sort, is unable to help. Nor should we forget that faithful love, in whatever area, implies, as the condition of possibility of its benefits, the possibility of guilt and shame in failure. By contrast, fickle love—the simulacrum of true love paraded and promoted in the Cave, paraded as shame and guilt free—is the root of many of our problems. It is in no way their solution, for in its essential infidelity it promotes the illusion that life can be satisfactorily lived entirely on one's whims. But with fidelity human love, for people and for institutions, remains as strong a bulwark as we have against the clashes of the night, the vagaries of fate and the inevitability of disappointment—all the things passed over in fantasies of drugs and experience machines.

The fact that these last few paragraphs are brief should not be taken to imply that love and fidelity are is less important than nature or toil. It is just that in talking of love, it is all too easy to be sentimental, the very thing we are attempting to avoid, and the more one talks the greater the danger.

AFTERWORD

The Silent Rock of Destiny

Many though not all aspects of our life resemble the situation of the prisoners in Plato's Cave. Insubstantial fanatasies are projected on to the walls of our Cave, displacing reality. Words do not mean what they say. We convince ourselves we can have what we want without cost.

All this is without malice or evil intention. Indeed much of our motivation is good, as are our aims. We desire not to hurt or offend. Nor is there anything wrong with happiness or pleasure or convenience or freedom or even, if properly construed, with self-esteem. But in this last proviso there is a huge qualification. There cannot be true self-esteem without self-worth, and self-worth has to be earned. Nor is there real happiness outside of a life well lived, of which happiness is the by-product. Pleasure, as opposed to happiness, actually becomes enervating and disabling of other, more important values if pursued exclusively and to their exclusion; while freedom is illusory if its exercise actually means the freedom to be succumb to the tyranny of one's desire and appetite. Indeed, the illusion that freedom consists in mastery by rather than of one's instincts is precisely that from which we should liberate ourselves.

Common to many of our characteristic illusions and failings there is a question of what philosophers call direction of fit. Our contemporary culture assumes that the world and our institutions must be made to fit our desires, and almost that the mere existence of a strong desire, individual or collective, creates an obligation that it be satisfied. Obviously such an impulse drives much technology, which becomes an unrelenting drive to make the world fit our material desires.

One can indeed argue about the extent to which scientific technology manifests impiety towards the natural world, and as such corrupts the souls of those of us who are driving the technology. But more insidious than science in this sense is the technology of the soul: the assumption that the main task of life is to allow the individual personality untrammelled expression and to accord it untrammelled satisfaction.

By contrast, in the words of C.S. Lewis, 'for the wise men of old the cardinal problem had been how to conform the soul to reality, and the solution had been knowledge, self-discipline and virtue'. We make ourselves fit reality, rather than the other way about.

But, it will be said, why should we, in the twenty-first century, conform the soul to reality? Why, when we have the ability to conform reality to the soul, should we be shipwrecked on the shoals of reality? Why should we not seek pleasure, happiness and ease, if such things are available, without beating our heads about a reality which cares not for us, and which does nothing for us?

This book has been an attempt to approach this question, but by the roundabout way of describing aspects of our lives in which, whether we know it or not, we are attempting to circumvent reality, and in the last three chapters, aspects in which reality breaks through our fantasies.

In lyrical or dramatic form our theme is well captured by the poet Hölderlin in his novel *Hyperion*:

'Heart's wave could not curl and break beautifully into the foam of spirit, unless the ageless, silent rock of destiny stood in its path.'

It is only against reality, and its adamantine hardness and incisiveness, that we fulfil anything of our true nature. Without interplay with a reality outside of ourselves, individually and collectively, celebrity is empty, happiness an illusion, achievement impossible, politics no more than a parade of impotent velleities, and a life of pleasure and ease an ultimate and frustrating deception. Unable to bear either silence or the hardness of reality, we are in the state so memorably captured by Pascal in his discussion of diversion.

Sometimes, when I set to thinking about the various activities of men, the dangers and troubles which they face at Court, or in war, giving rise to so many quarrels and passions, daring and often wicked enterprises and so on, I have often said that the sole cause of man's unhappiness is that he does not know how to stay quietly in his room.' The seeker of diversion cannot bear very much reality; he seeks activity, continual and empty activity, so as to divert himself. Thus people actually enjoy being superintendent, chancellor, chief justice, etc., not because of anything which is achieved in these offices, but just because a great number of people come to them from all over the place, 'and do not leave them a single hour of the day to think about themselves.

Such people (and academic life is full of them) nowadays make a fetish of going on almost invariably useless committees, trying to force others with better things to do to join them in wasting their time as well, and then complain endlessly about 'the burdens' of administration. And not just in academic life. Everywhere, one suspects, there are people whose lives are so impoverished that they need to fill them with useless but important seeming busyness. Despite what they say, they need it. Insignificant toil (if ever toil was insignificant) thus becomes an end in itself.

Pascal says similar things about those who spend all day chasing a hare they would never have thought of buying, about gamblers, about show-off dancers, and much else besides. To tell these people that what they are doing is futile or pointless is not just beside the point. It is actually wrong, because the point of what they are doing is the doing itself, not the ostensible goal of the activity.

Much of what Pascal says could be applied to our current fantasies, including our media driven celebrity culture. Human nature does not change. It simply finds different ways of expressing its basic condition. It is just that in a culture such as ours, with such degrees of surplus, diversion is ever more prominent and takes up more and more of our lives than ever before, which is not to say that we would all be better off being seventeenth century peasants in Europe during the Thirty Years War. Most of us today are to a greater or less extent in the condition of those courtiers at the court of Louis XIV who spent their lives busily waiting around all day doing absolutely nothing of any substance—but busily, note— with the difference that with us there is no King forcing us. While that style of life is easier and more pleasant than that of a peasant, it has its own multifarious discontents, only too evident to the eyes of a Pascal.

Pertinent as part of Pascal's diagnosis might seem to us today, however, we would find it very hard to accept in its entirety. We have two secret instincts, he says. One drives us endlessly to seek unreality in external diversion, which is both cause and result of our endless sense of wretched-ness, which, we might say no celebrity status or experience machine will assuage. The other, 'left over from the greatness of our original nature', tells us that the only true happiness lies in rest, not in excitement. But not, according to Pascal, in any old rest, but only in the rest which comes from acknowledging that our true salvation is to be found only in conversion, not just to God in some abstract sense, but in and through the person of Christ, God's Incarnate Son.

Pascal is in many ways a sceptic. He uses his considerable powers of reasoning to disparage human nature in general and human reason in particular, a somewhat paradoxical endeavour, some might feel. But having disparaged ordinary human life in general, including even the quite natural affection we have characterised as faithful love, Pascal is able to see only our ultimate wretchedness (our ever unquenchable quest for diversion)—and our ultimate greatness, which is salvation in Christ. As with his mentor, St Augustine, for Pascal, all of human life which is not to do with salvation is diversion or worse. In his negative point he agrees with Andy Warhol and the exponents of modern meaninglessness. Failing the sublimity of Christian spirituality, there is only the contemporary dross of celebrity and the mass media and of modern life more generally. There is nothing in between. So, to put it as starkly as possible, without serious religion, we are condemned to life in the Cave.

Pascal and Augustine may be right in thinking that

religion is what we are all looking for, whether we know it or not. And religion may still be what we are looking for, even if there is no truth in religion, and our quest doomed to disappointment. But it does not follow from this that without religion there is nothing but diversion. Not everything Pascal characterises as such is mere diversion. Some of what he criticises involves true engagement with realities not of our making, from which true fulfilment might spring.

Pascal and the moralists are right to point to the ultimate delusions of diversions which are not rooted in reality, or which take us from reality. And it is surely true that much of contemporary life is dominated by insistent fantasies and illusions, whose goal and net effect is diversion in Pascal's sense, with all the discontent and desperation that engenders. But, I have tried to suggest in the preceding three chapters, we can be saved from the fantasies and diversions of the Cave not only by Christianity (as Pascal would have it), but more mundanely by some quite ordinary realities of Middle Earth, as it were, such as a non-materialistic understanding of nature, fulfilment in significant toil and ordinary, and natural human love and piety. For most of us, our instinctive unhappiness with the Cave-like features of our lives, and with fantasies about drugs and experience machines comes with the contrast between them and what, deep down, we know about the true springs of human fulfilment.

To escape from the Cave, our immediate need is not a

religious conversion (even if that comes later), but a re-focusing on some basic truths, ordinary enough in themselves, but less exciting to articulate and harder to commit ourselves to than the seductive images flickering on the walls that surround us. As Plato's image suggests, all we need to do is to turn ourselves around from the wall and walk out of the Cave into the real world. But to paraphrase Eliot, this 'all', were we really to mean it, might be no less than everything. Plato himself saw a conversion of this sort—a turning away from the seductive fantasies thrown on to the walls of the Cave towards the true and the real—as the function of philosophy.

In the end we are all Plato's children. We may be in the Cave weighed down by the 'leaden weights' of food and similar pleasures and gluttonies, with which we are provided in the cave, and our minds filled with illusion and entertainment. Or we may 'suffer' (as Plato has it) a conversion towards the real and the true. Of course, a Platonic conversion will involve suffering, or at least hard yards, even if it also promises rewards greater than those of the Cave.

But we may take some consolation in the thought that the unhappiness with the illusions of the Cave, which we have examined in the first eleven chapters of this book, is predicated on a sense we still have that they are indeed illusions, and that life—our life, even in England, even in the twenty-first century—has more and better to offer.

ENDNOTES

1   In his book *Anarchy, State and Utopia* (Blackwell, 1974 pp 42-5).

2   Book 7 of *The Republic*.

3   *The Transformation of Intimacy: Sexuality, Love and Eroticism in Modern Societies* (1992).

4   Cf. Arthur C. Danto, 'The Philosopher as Andy Warhol' in *Philosophizing Art*, California, 1999, p 63).

5   Arthur C. Danto, *Beyond the Brillo Box*, New York, 1992, p 11.

6   *What Good Are the Arts?* London, 2005.

7   Cf. his 'Motivation and Readiness to Learn' in *Schools in the Learning Age*: edited by Bill Lucas and Toby Greany, London, 2000, pp 1-4.

8   Edited by Bill Lucas and Toby Greany, Campaign for Learning, 2000.

9   See Stephen J. Ball, 'Education, Majorism and the Curriculum of the Dead', *Curriculum Studies*, Vol 1 no 2, 1993, pp 195-213; and Margaret Brown, 'Clashing Epistemologies: the Battle for Control of the National Curriculum and its Assessment' inaugural lecture as Professor of Mathematics Education, King's College, London, 1993.

10   *Teachable Moments: the Art of Teaching in Primary Schools*, by Peter Woods and Bob Jeffrey, Buckingham, 1996, see Ch 7, esp pp 135 and 121-2.

11   Adam Phillips, *Darwin's Worms*, London, 1999, p115.

INDEX

Adam 203
Adenauer, Konrad 51
Adonis, Lord 140, 141
Aeneas 131, 156, 157, 214
Aeneid, The 155, 214
Africa 105, 106
AIDS 87, 88
America *see also USA* 36
American fundamentalists 102
Arnold, Matthew 222
Athens 12, 33
Augustine, St 230
Auschwitz 120
Austin, Jane 45
Ayer, Freddie 146
Ayres, Pam

Baader-Meinhof 98
Bacchus and Ariadne 156
Bach, Johan Sebastian 48
Back, Neil 191
Ball, Sir Christopher 109, 110,
    112, 128
Baker, Janet 74
BBC 44, 46, 125, 126, 214
Beethoven 48, 65, 66, 158, 159
Beckenbauer, Franz 54

Beckham, David 53, 54, 78, 192
Beckham, Victoria 71-75, 77, 78
Berlin Wall 22
Berlioz, Hector 155, 157, 159
Berry, Halle 48
Best 54
Best Bottom 2005 169
Bible, The 158
Big Brother 54, 68, 70, 72, 161
Birmingham 33
Blair, Tony 91, 95, 100, 101,
    102, 103
Blood, Mrs Diane 31, 32
Blunkett, David 127
Bob, Sir 106
Bouguereau 66
Bradley, F.H. 45, 66
Bradman, Don 51
Brahms, Johannes 208
Brave New World 41, 81, 82, 202
Britain 31, 103, 123
Bruckner, Anton 110

Caesar 125
Caliban 154
California 123
Cambridge 122, 138

Campaign for Learning 127, 128
Campbell, Naomi 53
Cantor, Georg 129
Capote, Truman 68
Carey, John 64-67,
Carlyle 208
Carter, Jimmy 90
Carthage 157
Celebrity Big Brother 47
Cézanne, Paul 61
China 106
Chopin, Frederic 208
Christ *see also Jesus* 230
Churchill 51
Clark, Kenneth
Clinton, Bill 56, 90
Coehlo, Paulo 66
Coleridge, Samuel Taylor 110
Compton, Denis
Congo 171, 212
Conrad 171, 205, 211, 212
Cosi Fan Tutte 155
Crewe, Quentin 151
Cruise, Tom 53, 56
Czechoslovakia 136

Dando, Jill 95
Dante 48, 130, 160
Danto, Arthur 62, 63, 67
Darcy, Mr 171
Darwin, Charles 110, 129, 164, 167
Dawkins, Richard 177, 180
Denmark 33
Dennett, Daniel 177
Dewey, John 108, 127
Deweyesque 109, 127, 128
Dickens, Charles 45, 131
Dickensian 145

Dido, Queen Sidonian 157
Disney, Walt 153
Disneyland 153
Durkheim, Emile 45
Duve, Christian de 200, 201
Dyke, Greg 46

EastEnders 46, 153
Einstein, Albert 67, 129
Elgar 110
Eliot, T.S. 66, 158, 232
Emin 66
Eminem 48
Encyclopedia Britannica 177
English National Opera Company 157
Faliraki 168, 169
Fein, Sinn 95, 96
Ferguson, Niall 177
Flintoff, Andrew 54
Foot and Mouth crisis 103
Freud, Sigmund 167
Garbo, Greta 52
Gaulle, de 51
Gay Science, The 112
GCSE 117-120, 147
Germany 168
Giddens, Anthony 26, 216
Gluck 74
Glyndebourne 155
Goldbach 110, 111
Greco, El 96
Greece 41, 125
Greek atomists 201

Handel, Georg Friedrich 74
Havel, Vaclav 136
Hegel 206
Hello 161
Hesiod 125

Hirst, Damien 48, 66
Hogarth, William 79
Hölderlin, Friedrich 227
Hollywood 153, 154
Holocaust 120
Homer 48, 125
Horace 126
Hume, David 19, 21, 202
Hummel 65
Hussein Saddam 102
Hutus 169
Huxley, Aldous 81-83
Hyperion 227

Ibiza 168
India 106
IRA 94, 95, 96
Iraq 100, 102, 103
Israeli right-wingers 102

Jackie (Onassis-Kennedy) 60, 62
Jackson, Michael 53
Jagger, Bianca 68
Jagger, Mick 67
Jesus 69, 96
John, Sir Elton 53
Johnson, Dr 69
Johnson, Martin 54, 191
Julian of Norwich 81

Kafka 110
Kant, Immanuel 158
Keats, John 131
Keble College 109
Kennedy, John F. 53, 54, 56, 58, 59
KLA 90
Kristallnacht 169

Laden, Osama bin 14
Larkin, Philip 34, 184
Learning to Fly 71
Leavis, F.R. 146
Leningrad 22
Lennon, John 53, 56, 69
Lepanto, the Battle of 96
Lewis C.S. 226
Live8 60, 104
Livy 126
London 22, 98, 155, 156, 161
London School of Economics 26
Louis XIV 229
Lucan 126
Lucretius 201

Macdonalds 211
Madonna 53
Majestik 171
Mallory, George 196
Manchester 22
Mao, Chairman 60, 62, 68
Marlow 211
Marxism 98
Matrix, The 7-10, 16
Matthews, Stanley
Media Studies 44, 122
Mendelssohn, Felix 208
Michelangelo 44, 61, 66, 160
Mill, J.S. 168
Milton, John 158, 203
Minelli, Liza 67
Ministry of Sound 171
Mittal affair 103
Monet, Claude 61
Monod, Jacques 200, 201, 202, 203
Monroe, Marilyn 53, 57, 58, 60, 62, 69

Monty 51
Moscow 22
Moses 160
Mosley, Sir Oswald 99
Moss, Kate 53, 79
Mowlam, Mo 94, 95
Mozart, Wolfgang Amadeus
    74, 155, 158, 159, 161
Muslim terrorists 102
Mussolini, Benito 99

Naples 155
National Gallery 156
Nazis 120
New Labour 85, 91, 92, 99, 216
Newton 129, 197-199, 202
Nietzsche, Friedrich 112, 167
Nobel prize 200
Nozick, Robert 8-10, 15

Oakesshott, Michael 49, 178
Oborne, Peter 103
OFSTED 147
Orwell, George 137
Ovid 126
Oxford 122, 138, 176, 177, 178

Paisley, Dr 95
Parry 208
Pascal, Blaise 110, 227-231
Patience Strong 66
Paul, St 169
Pele 54
Perret, Dominique 193, 194
Philip II, King 96
Phillips, Adam 167, 169
Picasso, Pablo 61
Pinker, Steven 177, 180
Pius XII, Pope 51
Plato 10, 12-17, 19, 29, 41, 43,

134, 176, 225, 232
Pliny 126
Pope, the 96
Popstars 54, 72
Presley, Elvis 53, 58, 60, 69
Proust, Marcel 66

Queen Elizabeth 86, 88, 91
Railtrack 103
Rake's Progress 80
Raphael 160, 203, 204
Red Brigade 98
Rees, Martin 177
Rembrandt 61
Rise of Political Lying, The 103
Robbins, Harold 66
Rolling Stones 48
Rome 125, 126, 214
Romeo and Juliet 155
Rousseau, Jean-Jacques 107,
    127, 185
Royal Opera House 138
Ruskin 45, 209, 210
Russell, Bertrand 202
Rwanda 169

Santayana, George 214
Schools in the Learning Age 127
Schubert, Franz 74
Schumann, Robert 74
Seneca 126
Serbs 102
Seutonius 126
Shakespeare, William 45, 131,
    153, 156
Simpson, Don 44
Simpson, Joe 194
Single Mothers by Choice 36
Smith, Adam 23
Socrates 12, 13, 110, 168

Soma 81, 82
Sony 48
Soviet 22, 139
Spencer, Earl 86
Spencer, Princess Diana 53, 56, 59, 69, 85-88, 90, 91, 95, 101
Spice Girls 71-73, 75, 76
Stalin 146
Stanford 208
Stendhal, Henri Beyle 160
Streisand, Barbra 67
Survivor 54, 70

Tacitus 126
Taylor, Elizabeth 53, 60, 67
Theory of the Leisure Class, The 185
Third Way, The 93, 94, 96, 99
Thirty Years War 229
Titian 66, 156, 158, 161
Trojans, The 155-157
Troy 157
Turkey 205
Turner, J.M.W. 48, 157, 206
Turner, Lana 68
Tutsis

Valentino, Rudolf

Veblen, Thorstein 185-187
Venus 157
Vettriano, Jack 66
Viet Cong 60
Vinci, Leonardo de 61
Virgil 48, 126, 156, 157, 214
Virtruvius 126

Ulster 94, 95
Ulster protestants 102
University of Derby 110
University of Durham 120, 124
USA 166

Warhol, Andy 53, 60-65, 67, 68, 75, 230
Waugh, Evelyn 37
Weber 45
White, Edmund 63
Who Wants to be a Millionaire? 54
Wickwire, Jim 194
Wilkinson, Jonny 191
Wittgenstein 48, 146, 215, 219
Wolf 74
Wordsworth 195, 196
Wordsworthian 197, 202
World War II 120